MOVIE SONGS
FOR SOLO FINGERSTYLE UKULELE
— 25 ARRANGEMENTS WITH TAB —

Arranged by
FRED SOKOLOW

Editorial assistance by Ronny S. Schiff

The following song is the property of:

Bourne Co.
Music Publishers
www.bournemusic.com

When You Wish Upon a Star

ISBN 978-1-70513-144-2

Visit Hal Leonard Online at
www.halleonard.com

World headquarters, contact:
Hal Leonard
7777 West Bluemound Road
Milwaukee, WI 53213
Email: info@halleonard.com

In Europe, contact:
Hal Leonard Europe Limited
1 Red Place
London, W1K 6PL
Email: info@halleonardeurope.com

In Australia, contact:
Hal Leonard Australia Pty. Ltd.
4 Lentara Court
Cheltenham, Victoria, 3192 Australia
Email: info@halleonard.com.au

TABLE OF CONTENTS

INTRODUCTION

Some of the songs in this collection are movie themes, such as "Song from M*A*S*H" and "Speak Softly, Love" (*The Godfather* Love Theme). Others are hit tunes that are irrevocably linked to a famous movie, like "As Time Goes By" (*Casablanca*) or "You've Got a Friend in Me" (in all the *Toy Story* films). All are beautiful, melodic songs, many of which won an Oscar or became a No. 1 hit. They're written by award-winning composers and translate wonderfully to ukulele.

Each song is arranged two ways:

- There's a chord/melody version – an instrumental arrangement in which you're playing chords and melody at the same time. This is one of the prettiest and most tuneful uses of the ukulele.

- There's a lead sheet with lyrics, chords, and chord grids, so you can sing the songs and strum a ukulele accompaniment, except for the two selections that are instrumentals with no lyrics.

There are also background and anecdotal stories about each song: who wrote it, in which film it appeared, and more.

Working your way through these arrangements, you'll undoubtedly find some new chord shapes. Besides learning 25 beautiful songs, you'll expand your chord vocabulary and begin to grasp the concept of how to arrange songs in the chord/melody style.

Enjoy!

Fred Sokolow

Fred Sokolow

As Time Goes By

from CASABLANCA

Words and Music by Herman Hupfeld

Written by Herman Hupfeld in 1931, its inclusion in the 1942 film, *Casablanca*, has made "As Time Goes By" one of the most iconic "movie songs" in cinematic history. It has become Warner Bros.' signature tune, and *Casablanca* is at the top of most "best movie" lists. In the film, the tune is sung by Dooley Wilson, and is used as a theme throughout the score.

As Time Goes By

from CASABLANCA

Words and Music by Herman Hupfeld

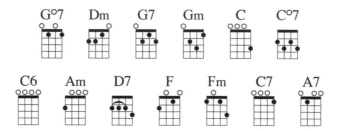

Verse 1
```
G°7 Dm            G7   Gm        G7    C        Dm  C°7 C6
```
You must remember this: a kiss is still a kiss, a sigh is just a sigh.
```
Am  D7          C°7 G7           C6 G°7
```
The fundamental things ap - ply, as time goes by.

Verse 2
```
G°7 Dm              G7   Gm          G7     C          Dm  C°7 C6
```
And when two lovers woo, they still say, "I love you," on this you can rely,
```
Am  D7          C°7 G7              C   F  Fm  C   C7
```
No matter what the future brings, as time goes by.

Bridge
```
F                        A7
```
Moonlight and love songs, never out of date.
```
Dm                 C°7
```
Hearts full of passion, jealousy and hate.
```
C             Am      D7
```
Woman needs man, and man must have his mate,
```
    G7   G°7  G7
```
That no one can deny.

Verse 3
```
G°7 Dm            G7   Gm            G7    C         Dm  C°7 C6
```
It's still the same old story, a fight for love and glory, a case of do or die.
```
Am  D7                      C    G°7 Dm G7 C  Fm   C
```
The world will always welcome lovers, as time goes by.

Can You Feel the Love Tonight

from THE LION KING
Music by Elton John
Lyrics by Tim Rice

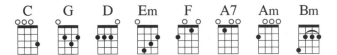

```
              C        G   C        G
Verse 1    There's a calm surrender to the rush of day,
              C        G         C         D
           When the heat of a rolling wind can be turned away.
              C        G   C        G
           An enchanted moment, and it sees me through.
              C           Em        F          D
           It's enough for this restless warrior just to be with you.


              G    D    Em   C  G    C    A7 D
Chorus     And can you feel the love tonight?   It is where we are.
              C  G       Em  D C       Am Bm C A7  D
           It's enough for this wide-eyed wanderer that   we got this far.
              G    D    Em   C  G          C  A7 D
           And can you feel the love tonight?   How it's laid to  rest!
              C  G       Em  D C         Am Bm C   G
           It's enough to make kings and vagabonds believe the  very best.


              C        G    C        G
Verse 2    There's a time for everyone, if they only learn
              C        G        C          D
           That the twisting kaleidoscope moves us all in turn.
              C        G   C        G
           There's a rhyme and reason to the wild outdoors,
              C            Em        F            D
           When the heart of this star-crosssed voyager beats in time with yours.


              G    D    Em   C  G    C    A7 D
Chorus     And can you feel the love tonight?   It is where we are.
              C  G       Em  D C       Am Bm C A7  D
           It's enough for this wide-eyed wanderer that   we got this far.
              G    D    Em   C  G          C  A7 D
           And can you feel the love tonight?   How it's laid to  rest!
              C  G       Em  D C         Am Bm C   G
           It's enough to make kings and vagabonds believe the  very best.
```

Can You Feel the Love Tonight

from THE LION KING
Music by Elton John
Lyrics by Tim Rice

This beautiful ballad, from 1994's *The Lion King*, was a collaboration between two "Sirs" — composer Sir Elton John and Sir Tim Rice, who also wrote lyrics for several Andrew Lloyd Webber blockbuster shows. Elton John's recording of the song became an international hit and won the Academy Award for Best Original Song in 1995.

Verse

Slow

Chorus

Beauty and the Beast

from BEAUTY AND THE BEAST
Music by Alan Menken
Lyrics by Howard Ashman

"Beauty and the Beast" is the theme song for the 1991 Disney film of the same name, written by
Howard Ashman and Alan Menken, who composed songs for many Disney films and other movie
and Broadway productions. Angela Lansbury sang "Beauty and the Beast" in the animated film.
A pop cover of the song by Celine Dion and Peabo Bryson helped launch Dion's career, and
inspired prominent singers to cover many songs from subsequent Disney films.

To Coda ✛

Bridge

11

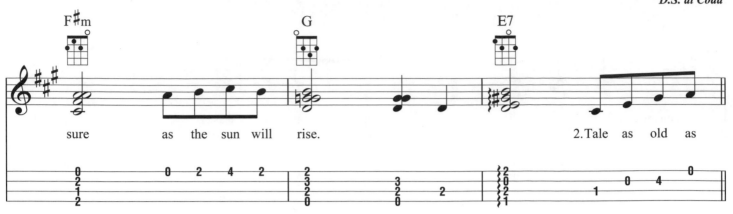

sure   as   the   sun   will   rise.   2.Tale   as   old   as

⊕ Coda

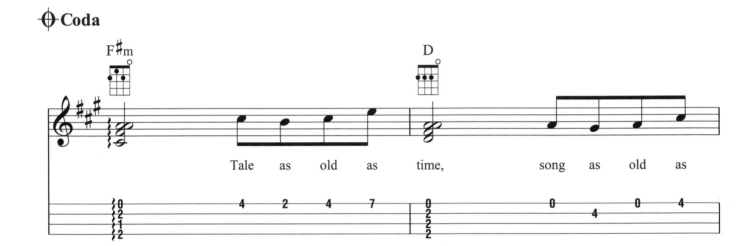

Tale   as   old   as   time,   song   as   old   as

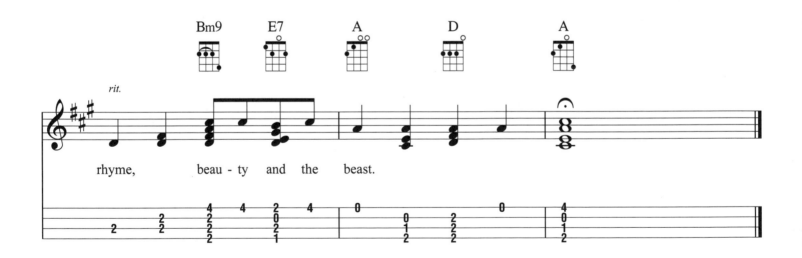

rhyme,   beau - ty   and   the   beast.

Beauty and the Beast

from BEAUTY AND THE BEAST
Music by Alan Menken
Lyrics by Howard Ashman

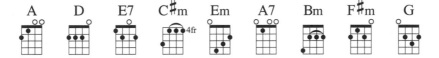

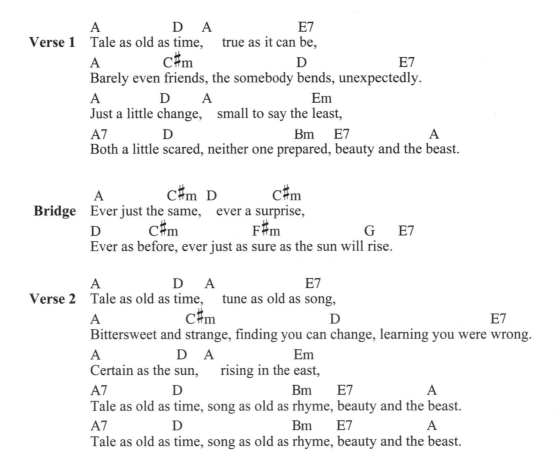

Verse 1
```
  A        D   A            E7
Tale as old as time,    true as it can be,
  A        C#m              D              E7
Barely even friends, the somebody bends, unexpectedly.
  A        D   A            Em
Just a little change,    small to say the least,
  A7       D                Bm   E7          A
Both a little scared, neither one prepared, beauty and the beast.
```

Bridge
```
  A          C#m D      C#m
Ever just the same,    ever a surprise,
  D        C#m            F#m              G   E7
Ever as before, ever just as sure as the sun will rise.
```

Verse 2
```
  A        D   A            E7
Tale as old as time,    tune as old as song,
  A        C#m              D                    E7
Bittersweet and strange, finding you can change, learning you were wrong.
  A        D   A            Em
Certain as the sun,    rising in the east,
  A7       D                Bm   E7          A
Tale as old as time, song as old as rhyme, beauty and the beast.
  A7       D                Bm   E7          A
Tale as old as time, song as old as rhyme, beauty and the beast.
```

City of Stars

from LA LA LAND
Music by Justin Hurwitz
Lyrics by Benj Pasek & Justin Paul

"City of Stars," featured in 2016's *La La Land*, was composed by Justin Hurwitz, with lyrics by Benj Pasek and Justin Paul. The song won an Oscar and a Golden Globe Award. Hurwitz had already scored other films and won other awards. Likewise, the team of Pasek and Paul had written lyrics for multiple films, television, and theater, including *James and the Giant Peach* and *The Greatest Showman*. Hurwitz said that, with "City of Stars," he "…went back and forth between cadencing in major and cadencing in minor," to capture the feeling of the wins and losses one can experience in show business in Los Angeles.

City of Stars

from LA LA LAND
Music by Justin Hurwitz
Lyrics by Benj Pasek & Justin Paul

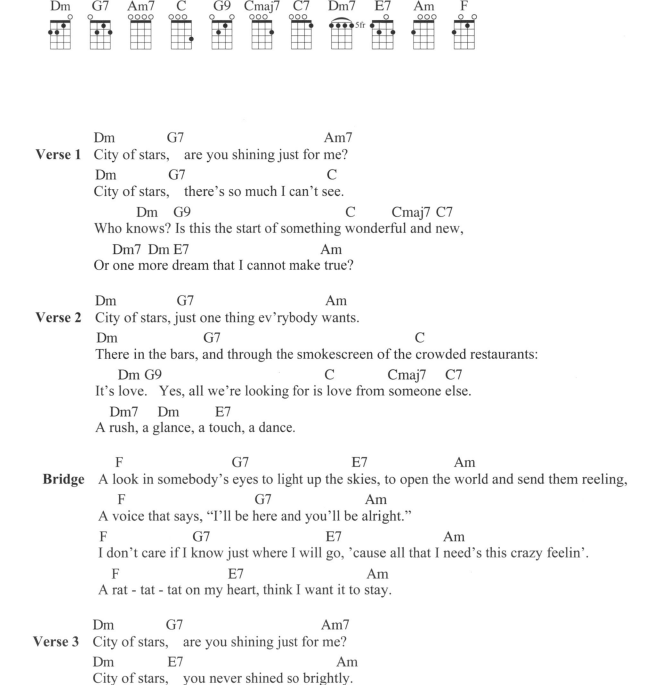

Verse 1

Dm   G7   Am7
City of stars,   are you shining just for me?

Dm   G7   C
City of stars,   there's so much I can't see.

Dm   G9   C   Cmaj7 C7
Who knows? Is this the start of something wonderful and new,

Dm7 Dm E7   Am
Or one more dream that I cannot make true?

Verse 2

Dm   G7   Am
City of stars, just one thing ev'rybody wants.

Dm   G7   C
There in the bars, and through the smokescreen of the crowded restaurants:

Dm G9   C   Cmaj7 C7
It's love. Yes, all we're looking for is love from someone else.

Dm7 Dm   E7
A rush, a glance, a touch, a dance.

Bridge

F   G7   E7   Am
A look in somebody's eyes to light up the skies, to open the world and send them reeling,

F   G7   Am
A voice that says, "I'll be here and you'll be alright."

F   G7   E7   Am
I don't care if I know just where I will go, 'cause all that I need's this crazy feelin'.

F   E7   Am
A rat - tat - tat on my heart, think I want it to stay.

Verse 3

Dm   G7   Am7
City of stars,   are you shining just for me?

Dm   E7   Am
City of stars,   you never shined so brightly.

Gabriel's Oboe

from the Motion Picture THE MISSION
Music by Ennio Morricone

Ennio Morricone, one of the greatest film composers, penned hundreds of movie and television scores and many classical works. First known for providing music for "spaghetti westerns" (filmed in Italy), Morricone went on to score films for some of the most esteemed directors of his time. He composed "Gabriel's Oboe" for the 1986's *The Mission*. It has been performed by many orchestras, and arrangements have been recorded by Yo-Yo Ma and other virtuoso instrumentalists.

Rubato throughout

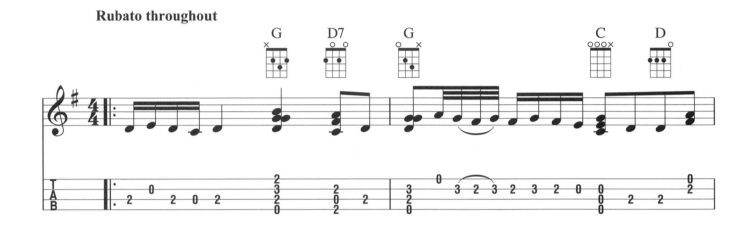

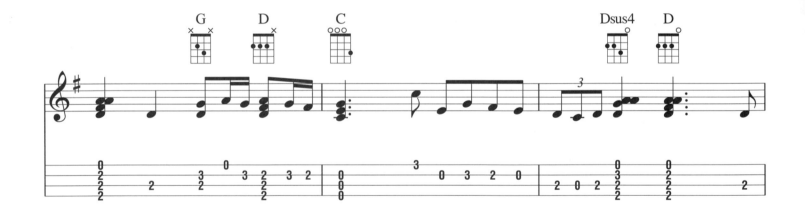

19

Hallelujah

featured in the DreamWorks Motion Picture SHREK
Words and Music by Leonard Cohen

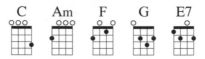

Verse 1
```
      C                      Am              C                Am
Well, I heard there was a secret chord that David played and it pleased the Lord,
      F           G          C      G
But you don't really care for music, do ya?
            C              F       G      Am             F
Well, it goes like this: the fourth, the fifth, the minor fall and the major lift.
      G           E7       Am      F        C         F        C G C
The baffled king composing hallelujah. Hallelujah, hallelujah, hallelujah, hallelu - jah.
```

Verse 2
```
            C                Am              C            Am
Your faith was strong, but you needed proof. You saw her bathing on the roof.
       F          G          C       G
Her beauty and the moonlight overthrew ya.
       C              F       G       Am                    F
She tied you to her kitchen chair, she broke your throne and she cut your hair,
       G            E7       Am      F        C         F        C G C
And from your lips she drew the hallelujah. Hallelujah, hallelujah, hallelujah, hallelu - jah.
```

Verse 3
```
      C            Am              C                 Am
Baby, I've been here before. I've seen this room and I've walked this floor.
      F         G          C      G
I used to live alone before I knew ya.
             C                 F       G      Am           F
And I've seen your flag on the marble arch, and love is not a victory march.
      G            E7       Am      F        C         F        C G C
It's a cold and it's a broken hallelujah. Hallelujah, hallelujah, hallelujah, hallelu - jah.
```

Verse 4

          C   Am   C   Am
There was a time when you let me know what's really going on below,

      F   G   C   G
But now you never show that to me, do ya?

        C   F   G   Am   F
But remember when I moved in you and the holy dove was moving too,

    G   E7   Am   F   C   F   C G C
And every breath we drew was hallelujah. Hallelujah, hallelujah, hallelujah, hallelu - jah.

Verse 5

          C   Am   C   Am
Maybe there's a God above. All I've ever learned from love

      F   G   C   G
Was how to shoot somebody who outdrew ya.

         C   F   G   Am   F
And it's not a cry that you hear at night, it's not somebody who's seen the light,

    G   E7   Am   F   C   F   C G C
It's a cold and it's a broken hallelujah. Hallelujah, hallelujah, hallelujah, hallelu - jah.

Hallelujah

featured in the DreamWorks Motion Picture SHREK
Words and Music by Leonard Cohen

Canadian singer/songwriter Leonard Cohen recorded "Hallelujah" in 1984. His record
company refused to release it as a single, but it was included on his *Various Positions* LP.
A few years later, Bob Dylan began performing it in concerts. John Cale recorded it in 1991,
and his version was included in the 2001 movie *Shrek*, garnering a huge audience for the song.
Jeff Buckley's 1994 version received critical acclaim, but did not become a hit until 2007,
ten years after his untimely death. Rufus Wainwright's later cover further popularized "Hallelujah,"
and to date it has been covered by over 300 artists and has been included in the soundtracks
of many movies and TV shows. (Cohen stated he wrote over 80 verses for the song initially,
and there are many alternate verses penned by other performers.)

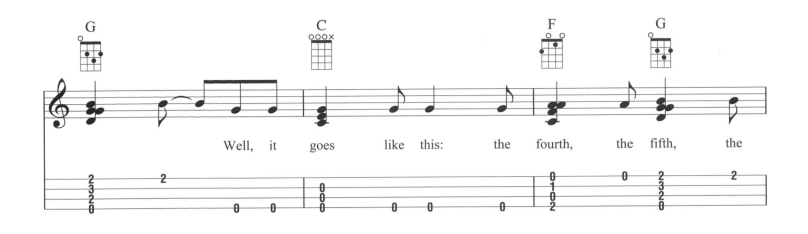

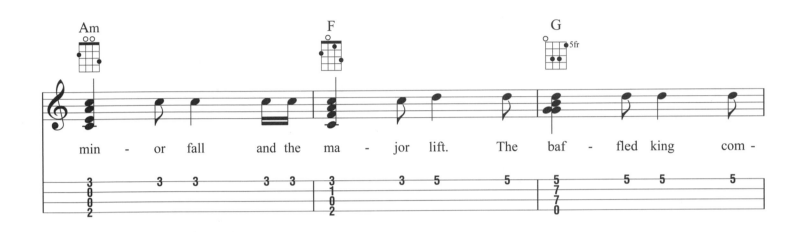

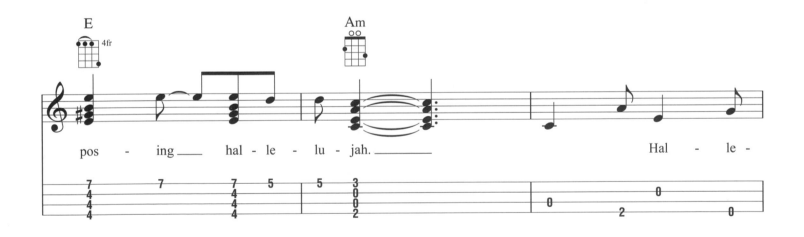

Hal - le - lu - jah,   hal - le -

lu   -   jah.

I Will Always Love You

featured in THE BODYGUARD
Words and Music by Dolly Parton

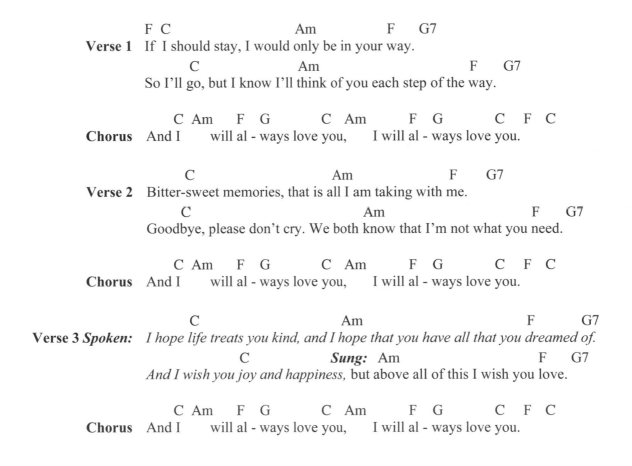

Verse 1
F C   Am   F   G7
If I should stay, I would only be in your way.
    C   Am   F   G7
So I'll go, but I know I'll think of you each step of the way.

Chorus
C Am   F G   C Am   F G   C F C
And I   will al - ways love you,   I will al - ways love you.

Verse 2
    C   Am   F   G7
Bitter-sweet memories, that is all I am taking with me.
    C   Am   F   G7
Goodbye, please don't cry. We both know that I'm not what you need.

Chorus
C Am   F G   C Am   F G   C F C
And I   will al - ways love you,   I will al - ways love you.

Verse 3 *Spoken:*
    C   Am   F   G7
I hope life treats you kind, and I hope that you have all that you dreamed of.
      C   ***Sung:*** Am   F   G7
And I wish you joy and happiness, but above all of this I wish you love.

Chorus
C Am   F G   C Am   F G   C F C
And I   will al - ways love you,   I will al - ways love you.

I Will Always Love You

featured in THE BODYGUARD

Words and Music by Dolly Parton

Dolly Parton scored a No. 1 hit twice with "I Will Always Love You": once in 1974, when it was first released, and again in 1982 when it was featured in the film *The Best Little Whorehouse in Texas*. She wrote it the same day she wrote her signature song, "Jolene." When Whitney Houston sang it in the 1992 film *The Bodyguard*, the song went to No. 1 again, and became one of the biggest-selling singles of all time.

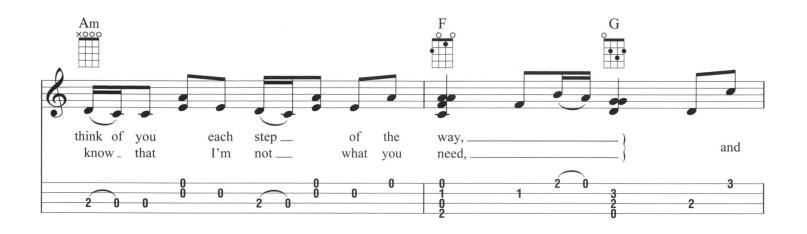

think of you   each step   of the   way, _____ } and
know _ that   I'm   not _   what you   need, _____

Chorus

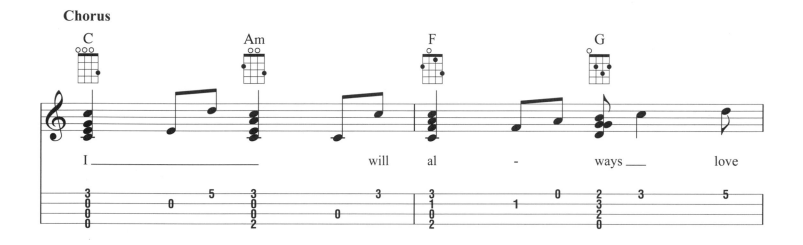

I _____   will   al   -   ways ___   love

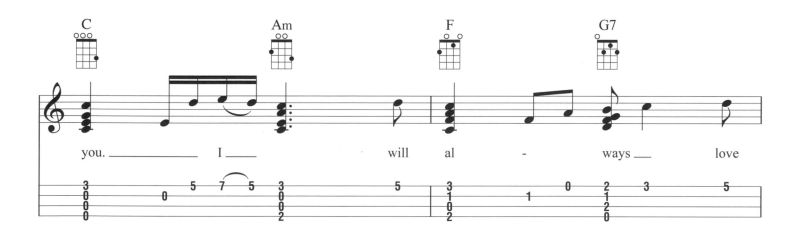

you. _____   I ___   will   al   -   ways ___   love

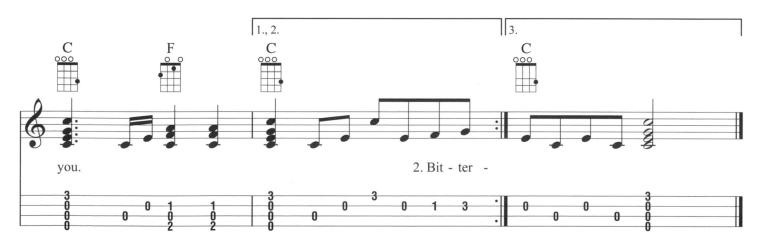

you.   2. Bit - ter -

Laura

from LAURA

Lyrics by Johnny Mercer
Music by David Raksin

David Raksin, composer of over 100 film scores and 300 television scores, wrote "Laura" for the 1945 film of the same name - a semi-noir, black-and-white murder mystery/romance story. Raksin composed the moody, haunting theme while processing a "Dear John" letter from his wife. Once the film became a hit, the illustrious Johnny Mercer, lyricist, composer of countless hits and co-founder of Capitol Records, wrote words to "Laura." The resulting song has become a jazz standard, and has been recorded by some of the most renowned vocalists - including Frank Sinatra, Nat "King" Cole, Tony Bennett, and Ella Fitzgerald.

sum - mer night,   that you can nev - er quite

D.C. al Coda

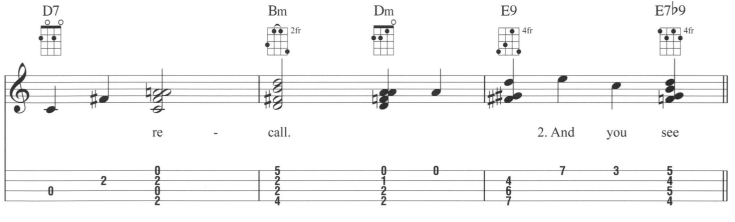

re - call.   2. And you see

Coda

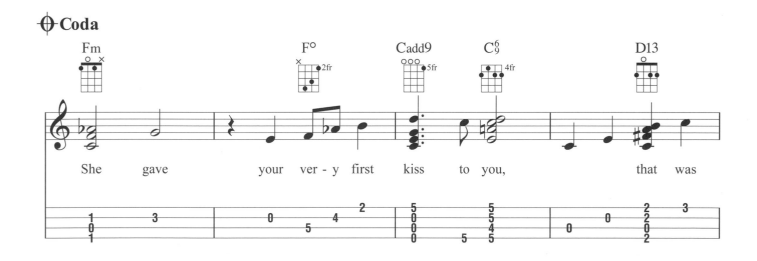

She gave your ver - y first kiss to you,   that was

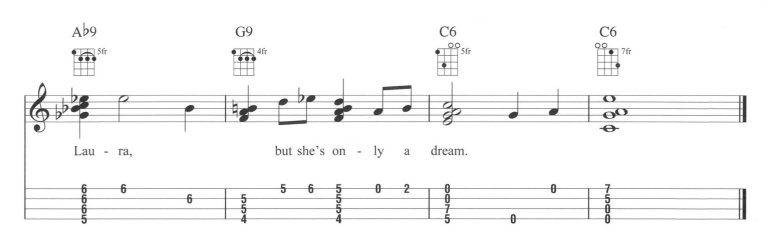

Lau - ra,   but she's on - ly a dream.

Laura

from LAURA

Lyrics by Johnny Mercer
Music by David Raksin

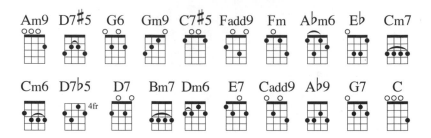

Am9   D7#5   G6   Gm9   C7#5   Fadd9   Fm   Abm6   Eb   Cm7

Cm6   D7b5   D7   Bm7   Dm6   E7   Cadd9   Ab9   G7   C

	Am9	D7#5	G6
Verse 1	Laura is the face in the misty light,		

Gm9   C7#5   Fadd9
Footsteps   that you hear down the hall.

Fm   Abm6   Eb
The laugh that floats on a summer night,

Cm7   Cm6 D7b5 D7 Bm7   Dm6
That you can never quite   re - call.

	E7	Am9	D7#5	G6
Verse 2	And you see Laura on the train that is passing through.			

Gm9   C7#5   Fadd9
Those eyes,   how familiar they seem.

Fm   Cadd9
She gave your very first kiss to you,

D7   Ab9   G7   C
That was Laura, but she's only a dream.

Moon River

from the Paramount Picture BREAKFAST AT TIFFANY'S
Words by Johnny Mercer
Music by Henry Mancini

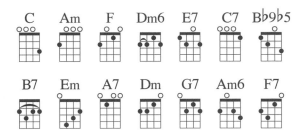

Verse 1
```
        C    Am    F         C
Moon river, wider than a mile,
        F              C        Dm6
I'm crossin' you in style, some day.
E7   Am    C7        F     Bb9b5
Old dream maker, you heartbreaker,
          Am         B7       Em A7       Dm  G7
Whevever you're goin', I'm go - in' your way.
```

Verse 2
```
        C    Am    F         C
Two drifters, off to see the world.
               F         C        Dm6
There's such a lot of world to see.
E7   Am  C7     Am6 F7        C
We're af - ter the same rainbow's end,
F                   C
Waitin' 'round the bend,
F              C       Am   Dm G7    C  Dm  C
My huckleberry friend, Moon River    and me.
```

Moon River

from the Paramount Picture BREAKFAST AT TIFFANY'S

Words by Johnny Mercer
Music by Henry Mancini

Henry Mancini, composer for countless films, has won four Academy Awards and 20 Grammy Awards. He is especially remembered for "The Pink Panther Theme," "Days of Wine and Roses," and "Moon River." The latter was written for the 1962 film, *Breakfast at Tiffany's*. Put Mancini's composition together with Johnny Mercer's lyrics, and it's no wonder "Moon River" won Oscar and Grammy awards and became a timeless standard, recorded by Frank Sinatra, Judy Garland, Louis Armstrong, Sarah Vaughan, Barbra Streisand, and many other notable vocalists.

Let It Go

from FROZEN
Music and Lyrics by Kristen Anderson-Lopez and Robert Lopez

"Let it Go" - written by husband-and-wife team Kristen Anderson-Lopez and Robert Lopez for 2013's *Frozen* - became a huge pop hit and won an Academy Award. Robert Lopez is one of the few artists who has won an Emmy, a Grammy, an Oscar, and a Tony award. The composing team was well aware that their songs for *Frozen* would be the first major musical experience for an entire generation of children.

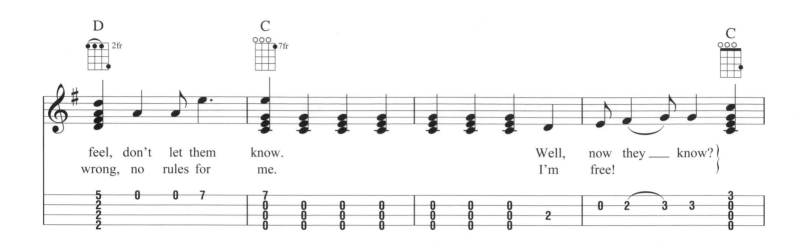

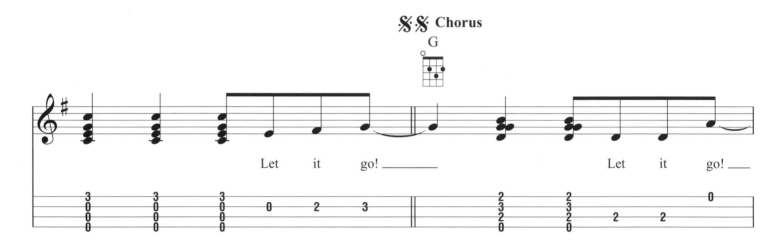

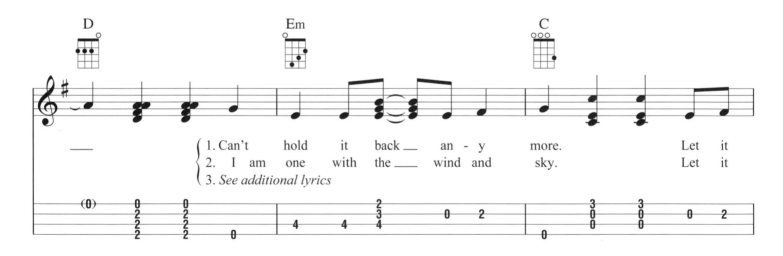

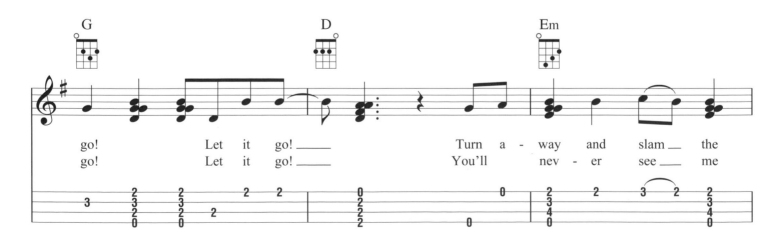

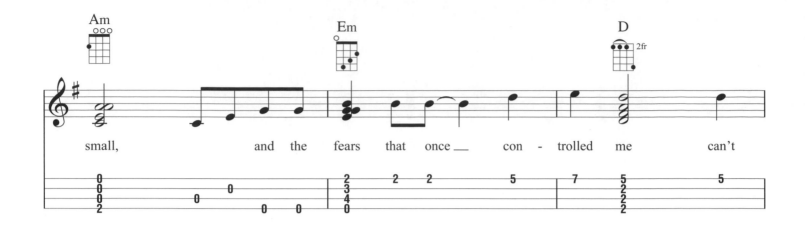

small,   and the   fears   that   once __   con - trolled   me   can't

D.S. al Coda 1

get   to   me ____   at   all.

⊕ **Coda 1**

Bridge

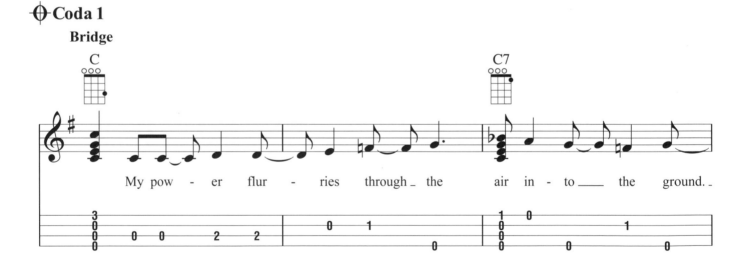

My   pow -   er   flur - ries   through __   the   air   in - to ____   the   ground.

____   My   soul __   is   spi - ral - ling ____   in

38

fro - zen frac - tals all a - round. ___ And one ___ thought crys -

- tal - liz - es like an ic - y blast. ___

I'm nev - er go - ing back, ___ the past is in ___ the

D.S.S. al Coda 2 ⊕ **Coda 2**

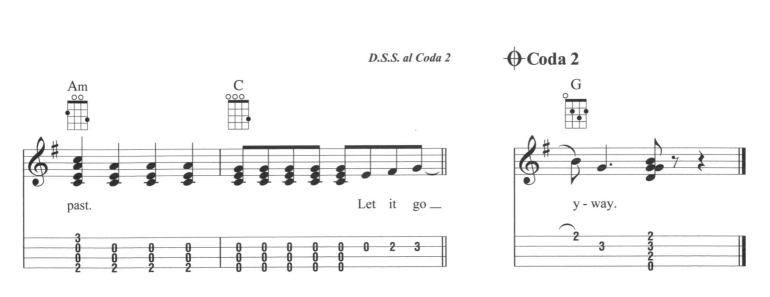

past.   Let it go ___   y - way.

Let It Go

from FROZEN

Music and Lyrics by Kristen Anderson-Lopez and Robert Lopez

Em Cmaj7 D Am C G Bm B♭ C7 E

Verse 1
        Em   Cmaj7   D   Am
The snow glows white on the mountain tonight, not a footprint to be seen.
       Em   C   D   Am
A kingdom of isolation, and it looks like I'm the Queen.
Em   C   D   Am
The wind is howling like this swirling storm inside.
Em   D   A
Couldn't keep it in, heaven knows I've tried.

Pre-Chorus 1
D   C   D
Don't let them in, don't let them see. Be the good girl you always have to be.
                       C
Conceal, don't feel, don't let them know. Well, now they know!

Chorus 1
        G   D   Em   C
Let it go! Let it go! Can't hold it back anymore.
        G   D   Em   C
Let it go! Let it go! Turn away and slam the door.
G   D   Em   C
I don't care what they're going to say.
        Bm   B♭   C   G
Let the storm rage on. The cold never bothered me anyway.

Verse 2
        Em   Cmaj7   D   Am
It's funny how some distance makes everything seem small,
       Em   D   A7
And the fears that once controlled me can't get to me at all.

Pre-Chorus 2
D   C   D
It's time to see what I can do, to test the limits and break through.
                       C
No right, no wrong, no rules for me, I'm free!

Chorus 2
        G   D   Em   C
Let it go! Let it go! I am one with the wind and sky.
        G   D   Em   C
Let it go! Let it go! You'll never see me cry.
G   D   Em   C
Here I stand, and here I'll stay.
        Bm   B♭   C   G
Let the storm rage on. The cold never bothered me anyway.

```
               C                           C7        C
Bridge    My power flurries through the air into the ground.
                               C7
          My soul is spiraling in frozen fractals all around.
          D                           D7        D
          And one thought crystallizes like an icy blast.
          E        Cmaj7          D           Am   C
          I'm never going back, the past is in the past.


               G        D       Em                  C
Chorus 3   Let it go! Let it go, and I'll rise like the break of dawn.
               G        D       Em          C
           Let it go! Let it go! That perfect girl is gone.
          G    D         Em    C
          Here I stand, in the light of day.
              Bm        B♭     C                     G
          Let the storm rage on. The cold never bothered me anyway.
```

A Million Dreams

from THE GREATEST SHOWMAN

Words and Music by Benj Pasek and Justin Paul

Benj Pasek and Justin Paul (see "City of Stars") wrote "A Million Dreams" for the 2017 film *The Greatest Showman*. It's sung by Hugh Jackman and Michelle Williams in the movie, and Pink, Susan Boyle, and other renowned vocalists have recorded it as well. Both the film and soundtrack album were global successes, and "A Million Dreams" has well over a 100 million views on YouTube.

I don't care,   I don't care,   so   call   me
I don't care,   I don't care if they   call   us

cra - zy.
cra - zy.

We   can   live   in   a
Run   a - way   to   a

world   that   we ____   de - sign. ____

'Cause

𝄋 Chorus

ev - 'ry   night ____   I   lie ____   in   bed, ____   the   bright - est   col - ors

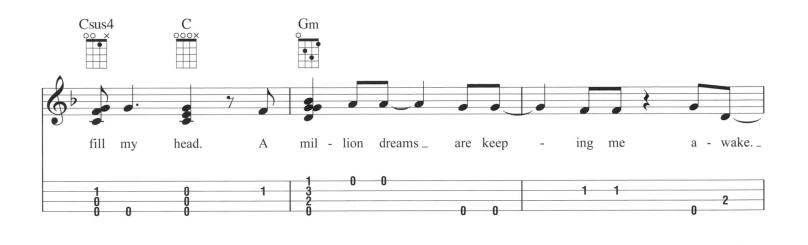

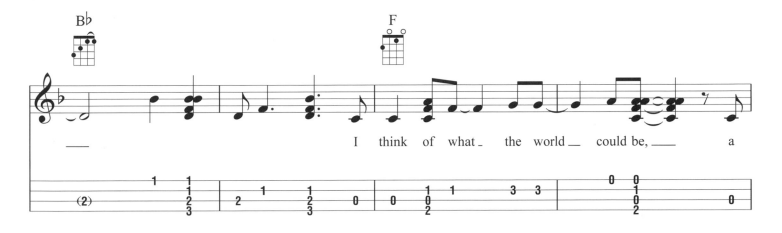

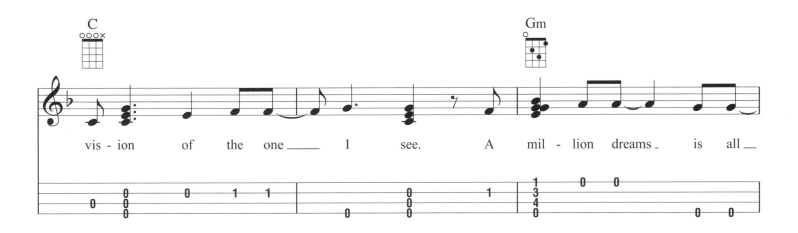

To Coda ⊕

A Million Dreams

from THE GREATEST SHOWMAN

Words and Music by Benj Pasek and Justin Paul

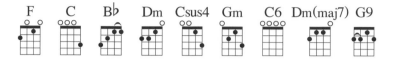

Verse 1

     F   C   Bb   F   C   Bb
I close my eyes and I can see the world that's waiting up for me that I call my own.
     F   C   Bb   F   C   Bb
Through the dark, through the door, through where no one's gone before, but it feels like home.

Pre-Chorus 1

C   Dm C   Bb F C   Dm   C   Bb
They can say, they can say it all sounds crazy. They can say, they can say I've lost my mind.
C   Dm   C   Bb C   Bb   C   Bb
I don't care, I don't care, so call me crazy. We can live in a world that we design.

Chorus 1

           F   C   Csus4 C
'Cause every night I lie in bed, the brightest colors fill my head.
   Gm   Bb
A million dreams are keeping me awake.
     F   C
I think of what the world could be, a vision of the one I see.
   Gm   Bb   F
A million dreams is all it's gonna take. Oh, a million dreams for the world we're gonna make.

Verse 2

     F   C   Bb   F   C   Bb
There's a house that we can build, every room inside is filled with the things from far away.
     F   C   Bb   F   C6 Bb
Special things I compile, each one there to make you smile on a rainy day.

Pre-Chorus 2

C   Dm C   Bb F C   Dm   C   Bb
They can say, they can say it all sounds crazy. They can say, they can say we've lost our minds.
C   Dm   C   Bb C   Bb   C   Bb
I don't care, I don't care if they call us crazy. Runaway to a world that we design.

Chorus 2   **Repeat Chorus 1**

Bridge
```
Dm        Dm(maj7)     F            G9        Bb                      F
```
However big, however small, let me be part of it all. Share your dreams with me.
```
Dm          Dm(maj7)       F                    G9        Bb      C       F
```
You may be right, you may be wrong, but say that you'll bring me along to the world you see,
```
        C            Bbmaj7           F      C7
```
To the world I close my eyes to see, I close my eyes to see.

Chorus 3
```
            F                     C              Csus4  C
```
'Cause every night I lie in bed, the brightest colors fill my head.
```
  Gm                       Bb
```
A million dreams are keeping me awake.
```
  F                        C
```
I think of what the world could be, a vision of the one I see.
```
  Gm                       Bb                               F    C
```
A million dreams is all it's gonna take. Oh, a million dreams for the world we're gonna make,
```
F                      C  Bb
```
For the world we're gonna make.

My Heart Will Go On

(Love Theme From 'Titanic')

from the Paramount and Twentieth Century Fox Motion Picture TITANIC
Music by James Horner
Lyric by Will Jennings

James Horner, composer of over 100 film scores, wrote the music for *Titanic*, which has become the best-selling orchestral film score on record. Will Jennings was his lyricist for "My Heart Will Go On." Winner of multiple GRAMMY, Golden Globe, and Academy Awards, Jennings has penned lyrics for Eric Clapton ("Tears in Heaven"), Whitney Houston, B.B. King, Jimmy Buffett, Roy Orbison, and Stevie Winwood. Celine Dion's recording topped the pop charts in over 20 countries, becoming her signature song and one of the best-selling singles of all time. Like other James Horner melodies, the tune has a Celtic feel.

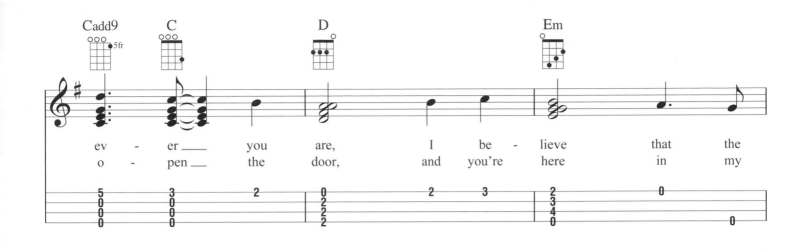

ev - er ____ you are, I be - lieve that the
o - pen ____ the door, and you're here in my

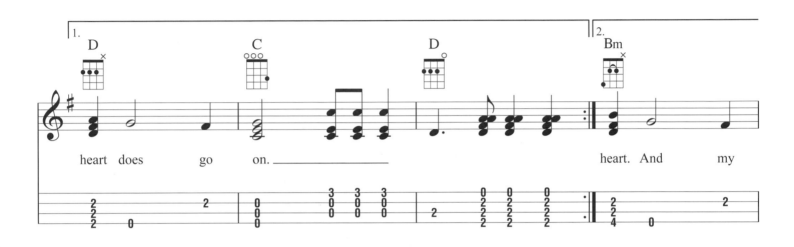

heart does go on. ____ heart. And my

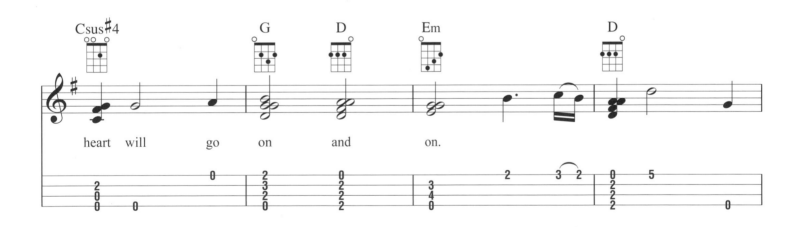

heart will go on and on.

To Coda ✛   1st time, D.C.
(take repeats)
2nd time, D.S. al Coda
(take repeat)   ✛ Coda

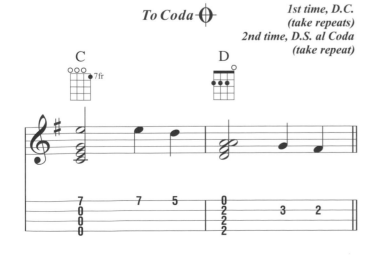

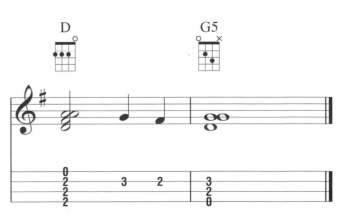

My Heart Will Go On

(Love Theme From 'Titanic')

from the Paramount and Twentieth Century Fox Motion Picture TITANIC

Music by James Horner
Lyric by Will Jennings

G   Dsus4   C   D   Gsus4   Em   Bm   G5

Verse 1
G   Dsus4   C   G D G   Dsus4   Gsus4 D
Ev'ry night in my dreams, I see you, I feel you. That is how I know you go on.
G   Dsus4   C   G   D G   Dsus4   Gsus4   D
Far across the distance and spaces between us, you have come to show you go on.

Chorus 1
Em D   C   D   Em   D   C D
Near, far, wherev - er you are, I believe that the heart does go on.
Em D   C   D   Em   Bm   C   G D Em
Once more, you o - pen the door, and you're here in my heart. And my heart will go on and on.
D C D

Verse 2
G   Dsus4   C   G D   G   Dsus4   G D
Love can touch us one time and last for a life - time, and never let go 'til we're gone.
G   Dsus4   C   G D G   Dsus4   G D
Love was when I loved you, one true time I hold to. In my life we'll always go on.

Chorus 2
Em D   C   D   Em   D   C D
Near, far, wherev - er you are, I believe that the heart does go on.
Em D   C   D   Em   Bm   C   G D Em
Once more, you o - pen the door, and you're here in my heart. And my heart will go on and on.
D C D

Chorus 3
Em D   C   D   Em   D   C D
You're here, there's noth - ing I fear, and I know that my heart will go on.
Em D C   D   Em   Bm   C   G D Em
We'll stay forev - er this way. You are safe in my heart. And my heart will go on and on.
D   C D G5

The Rainbow Connection

from THE MUPPET MOVIE
Words and Music by Paul Williams and Kenneth L. Ascher

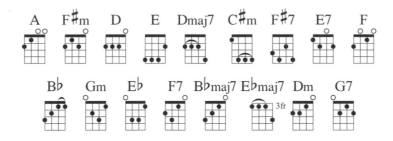

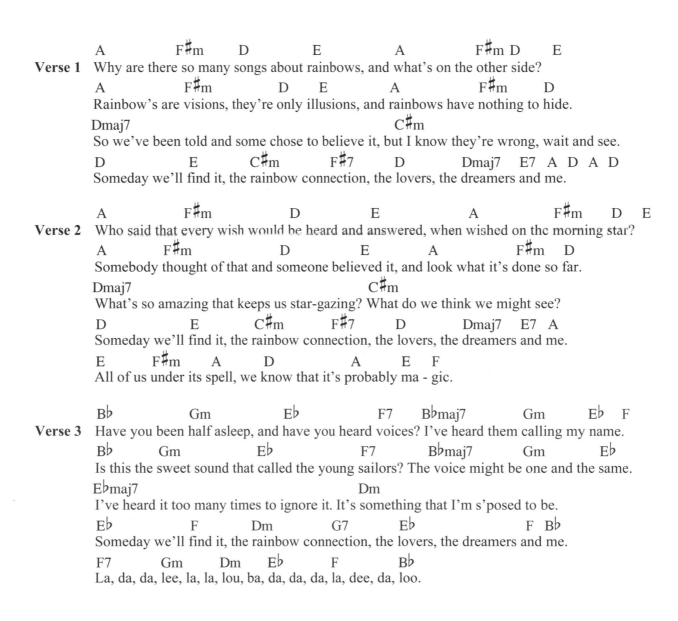

Verse 1

A   F#m   D   E   A   F#m D   E
Why are there so many songs about rainbows, and what's on the other side?

A   F#m   D   E   A   F#m   D
Rainbow's are visions, they're only illusions, and rainbows have nothing to hide.

Dmaj7   C#m
So we've been told and some chose to believe it, but I know they're wrong, wait and see.

D   E   C#m   F#7   D   Dmaj7 E7 A D A D
Someday we'll find it, the rainbow connection, the lovers, the dreamers and me.

Verse 2

A   F#m   D   E   A   F#m   D E
Who said that every wish would be heard and answered, when wished on the morning star?

A   F#m   D   E   A   F#m   D
Somebody thought of that and someone believed it, and look what it's done so far.

Dmaj7   C#m
What's so amazing that keeps us star-gazing? What do we think we might see?

D   E   C#m   F#7   D   Dmaj7 E7 A
Someday we'll find it, the rainbow connection, the lovers, the dreamers and me.

E   F#m   A   D   A   E   F
All of us under its spell, we know that it's probably ma - gic.

Verse 3

Bb   Gm   Eb   F7   Bbmaj7   Gm   Eb F
Have you been half asleep, and have you heard voices? I've heard them calling my name.

Bb   Gm   Eb   F7   Bbmaj7   Gm   Eb
Is this the sweet sound that called the young sailors? The voice might be one and the same.

Ebmaj7   Dm
I've heard it too many times to ignore it. It's something that I'm s'posed to be.

Eb   F   Dm   G7   Eb   F Bb
Someday we'll find it, the rainbow connection, the lovers, the dreamers and me.

F7   Gm   Dm   Eb   F   Bb
La, da, da, lee, la, la, lou, ba, da, da, da, la, dee, da, loo.

The Rainbow Connection

from THE MUPPET MOVIE
Words and Music by Paul Williams and Kenneth L. Ascher

Composer, arranger, and jazz pianist Kenneth Ascher collaborated with songwriter Paul Williams ("We've Only Just Begun," "Evergreen") for the second time when they wrote music for 1979's *The Muppet Movie*. The film begins with Kermit the Frog singing "The Rainbow Connection" while plucking a five-string banjo. The composers said they were inspired by "When You Wish Upon a Star" when writing "Rainbow Connection."

1. Why are there so man-y songs a-bout
   Rain bows are vis ions, they're on - ly il -
2. *See additional lyrics*

rain - bows, ___ and what's on the oth - er side?
lu - sions, ___ and rain - bows have noth - ing to hide.

So we've been told and some choose to be - lieve it, ___ but

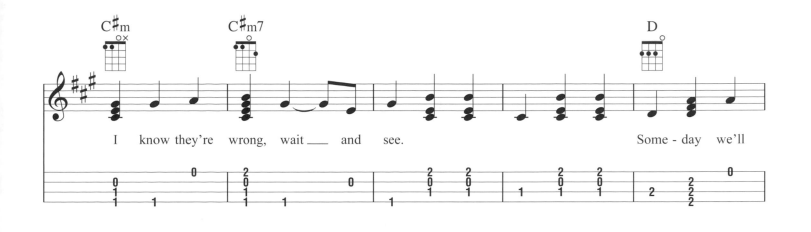

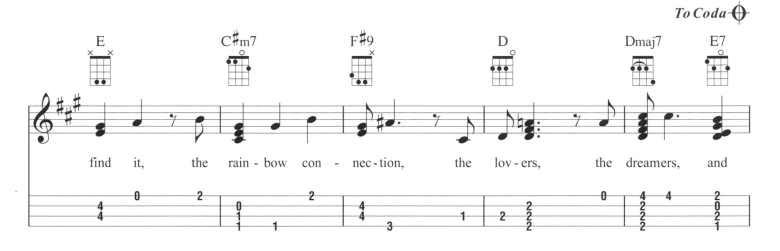

To Coda ⊕

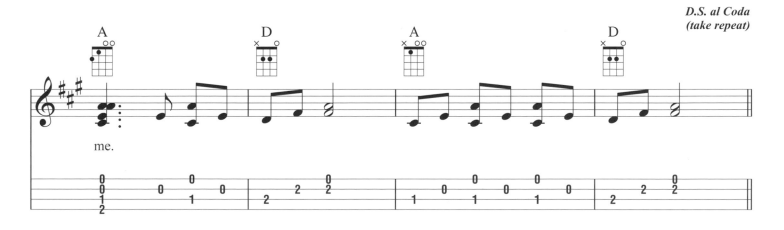

D.S. al Coda
(take repeat)

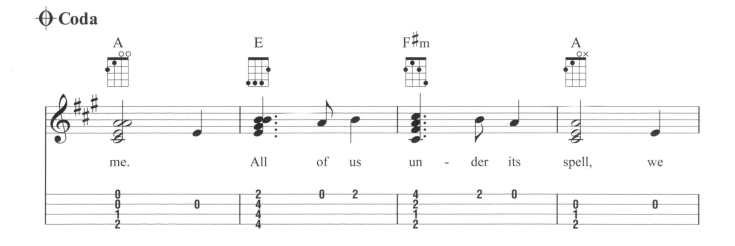

⊕ **Coda**

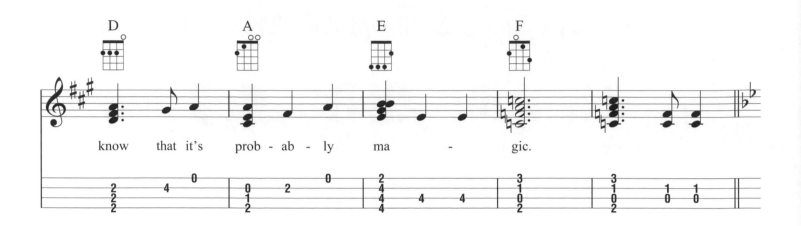

know that it's prob - ab - ly ma - gic.

Verse

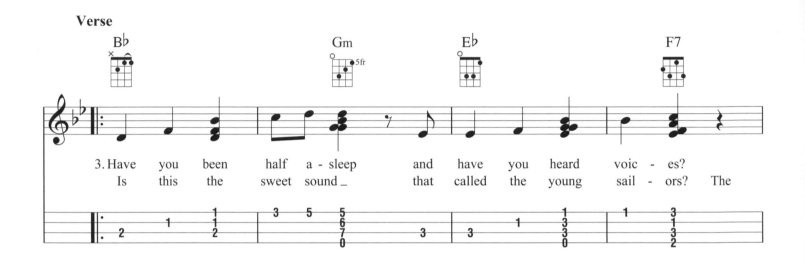

3. Have you been half a - sleep and have you heard voic - es?
Is this the sweet sound ___ that called the young sail - ors? The

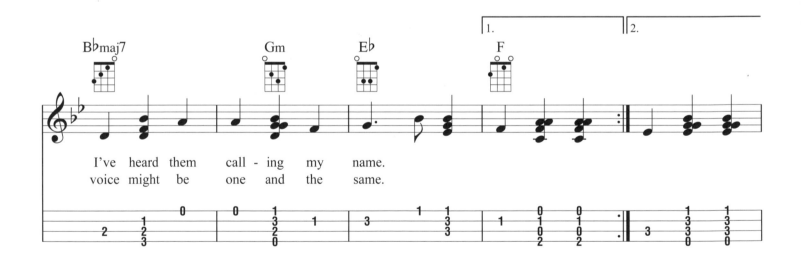

1.
2.

I've heard them call - ing my name.
voice might be one and the same.

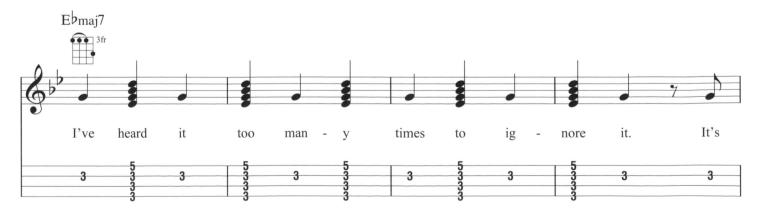

I've heard it too man - y times to ig - nore it. It's

Over the Rainbow

from THE WIZARD OF OZ
Music by Harold Arlen
Lyric by E.Y. "Yip" Harburg

Written by Harold Arlen and Yip Harburg for the 1939 classic film *The Wizard of Oz*,
"Over the Rainbow" became Judy Garland's signature song because of her unforgettable,
wistful performance in the movie. As a team, and individually, Arlen and Harburg composed
a long list of songs that have become standards in The Great American Songbook.
"Over the Rainbow" has enjoyed recent popularity because of Israel Kamakawiwo'ole's
1993 recording, which he played as a medley with "What a Wonderful World."

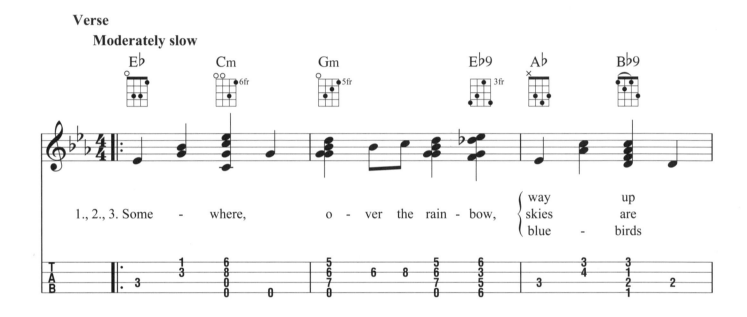

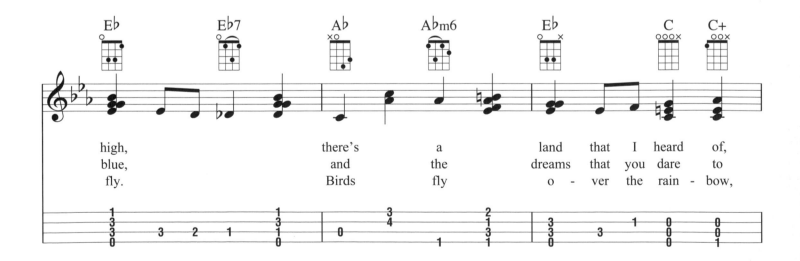

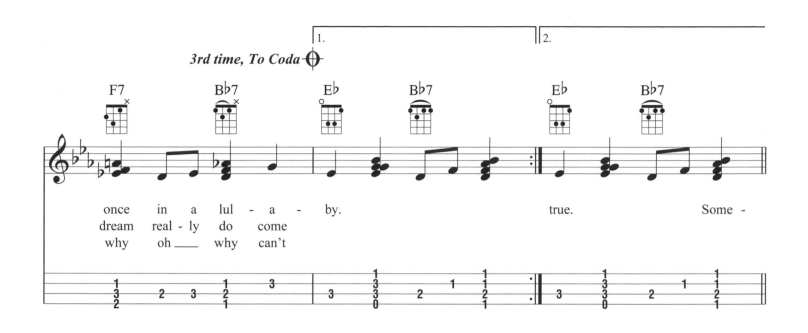

once in a lul - a - by.   true.   Some -
dream real - ly do come
why oh ___ why can't

Bridge

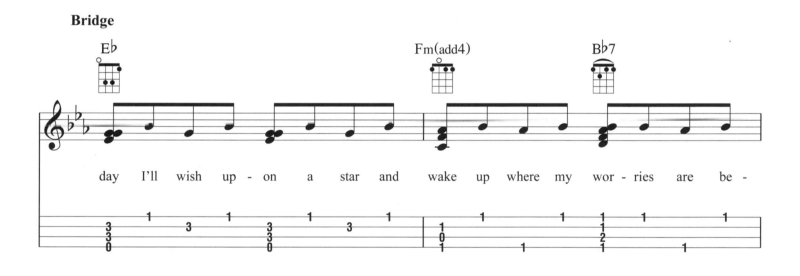

day I'll wish up - on a star and wake up where my wor - ries are be -

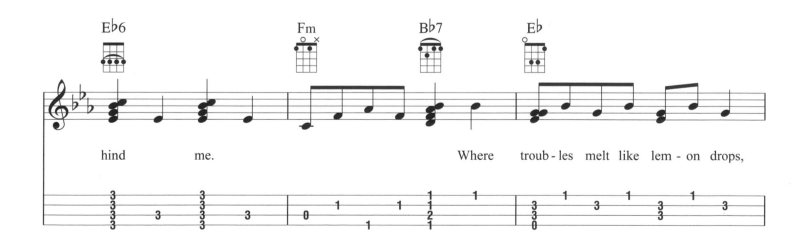

hind   me.   Where troub - les melt like lem - on drops,

way up on the chim-ney tops, that's where   you'll   find   me. _____

Coda

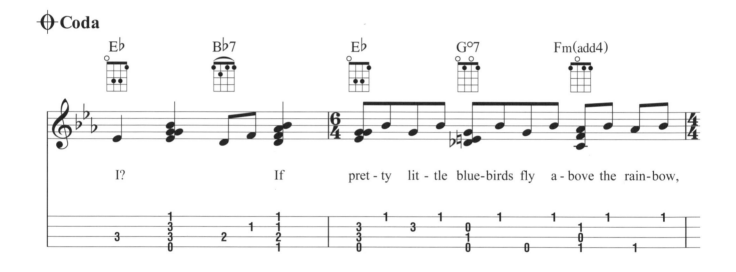

I?   If   pret-ty lit-tle blue-birds fly a-bove the rain-bow,

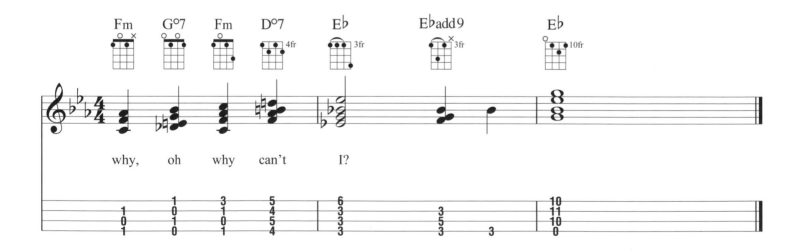

why,   oh   why can't   I?

Over the Rainbow

from THE WIZARD OF OZ
Music by Harold Arlen
Lyric by E.Y. "Yip" Harburg

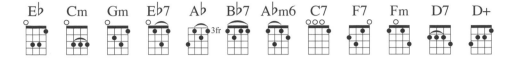

Verse 1
```
       Eb    Cm   Gm       Eb7  Ab Bb7 Eb Eb7
Some - where, over the rainbow, way  up   high,
       Ab   Abm6 Eb        C7      F7       Bb7  Eb Bb7
There's a      land that I heard of, once in a lulla - by.
```

Verse 2
```
       Eb    Cm   Gm       Eb7  Ab Bb7 Eb Eb7
Some - where, over the rainbow, skies are  blue,
       Ab   Abm6 Eb        C7      F7       Bb7   Eb Bb7
And the    dreams that you dare to dream really do come true.
```

Bridge
```
                  Eb                        Fm
Some day I'll wish upon a star and wake up where my
Bb7          Eb        Fm
Worries are behind me.
Bb7       Eb
Where troubles melt like lemon drops,
D7                                  Gm   D+   Fm Bb7
Way up on the chimney tops, that's where you'll find  me.
```

Verse 3
```
       Eb    Cm   Gm       Eb7  Ab Bb7 Eb Eb7
Some - where, over the rainbow, blue - birds fly.
       Ab   Abm6 Eb   C7      F7       Bb7   Eb Bb7
Birds fly     over the rainbow, why, oh why can't I?
       Eb                      Fm              Gm Ab Bb7 Eb
If  pretty little blue birds fly a - bove the rainbow, why, oh   why can't I?
```

Remember Me

(Ernesto de la Cruz)
from COCO
Words and Music by Kristen Anderson-Lopez and Robert Lopez

Once again, the Lopez couple (see "Let It Go") scored an Oscar for "Remember Me," the signature song of 2017's *Coco*. Performed several times in the movie, in many different styles, the song has won many awards. The composers listened to popular, older Mexican music in order to make "Remember Me" fit the genre implied by *Coco's* story line.

Remember Me

(Ernesto de la Cruz)
from COCO
Words and Music by Kristen Anderson-Lopez and Robert Lopez

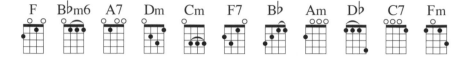

F   B♭m6   A7   Dm   Cm   F7   B♭   Am   D♭   C7   Fm

                        F   B♭m6
Verse 1   Remember me, thought I have to say goodbye,
                        F   B♭m6   A7
              Remember me. Don't let it make you cry.
                  Dm   Cm   F7
              For even if I'm far away, I hold you in my heart.
                  B♭   B♭m6   C7
              I sing a secret song to you each night we are apart.

                        F   B♭m6
Verse 2   Remember me, though I have to travel far,
                        F   F7
              Remember me, each time you hear a sad guitar.
                  B♭   Am   A7   Dm
              Know that I'm with you the only way that I can be.
                  D♭   C7   Fm D♭ B♭m6 F
              Until you're in my arms again, re - mem - ber me.

The Shadow of Your Smile

Love Theme from THE SANDPIPER
Music by Johnny Mandel
Words by Paul Francis Webster

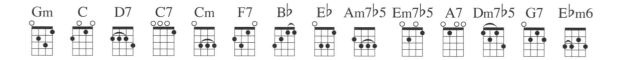

Gm   C   D7   C7   Cm   F7   B♭   E♭   Am7♭5   Em7♭5   A7   Dm7♭5   G7   E♭m6

Verse 1

Gm   C   D7   Gm
The shadow of your smile when you are gone

C7   Cm   F7   B♭
Will color all my dreams and light the dawn.

E♭   Am7♭5   D7   Gm
Look into my eyes, my love, and see

B♭   Em7♭5   A7   Am7♭5   D7
All the lovely things you are to me.

Verse 2

Gm   C   D7   Gm
Our wistful little star was far too high.

C7   Cm   F7   Dm7♭5   G7
A teardrop kissed your lips and so did I.

Cm   E♭m6   B♭   Dm7♭5   G7
Now when I remember spring, all the joys that love can bring,

C7   F7   B♭
I will be remembering   the shadow of your smile.

The Shadow of Your Smile

Love Theme from THE SANDPIPER

Music by Johnny Mandel
Words by Paul Francis Webster

Yet another Academy Award and Grammy-winning song, "The Shadow of Your Smile" was penned by Johnny Mandel, composer/arranger for dozens of films, television shows, and hit songs like "Suicide Is Painless" and "A Time for Love." Paul Francis Webster - of "Lara's Theme," "Secret Love," "Love Is a Many Splendored Thing," "A Certain Smile," and many other hits - provided the lyrics. The song debuted in *The Sandpiper*, a 1965 film starring Elizabeth Taylor and Richard Burton. Like many of the songs in this collection, it has become a jazz standard as well as a vehicle for some of the most famous pop vocalists (Johnny Mathis, Tony Bennett, Stevie Wonder, Frank Sinatra, and Barbra Streisand, to name a few).

Shallow

from A STAR IS BORN
Words and Music by Stefani Germanotta, Mark Ronson, Andrew Wyatt and Anthony Rossomando

Lady Gaga and three other notable rock/pop performers/songwriters (Andrew Wyatt, Anthony Rossomando, and Mark Ronson) composed "Shallow," the Academy Award-winning song featured three times in the 2018's *A Star Is Born*. The references to water and diving came about because the original script had Bradley Cooper's character drown, as James Mason did in a 1954 incarnation of the film. There have been four *Star Is Born* movies, all of which tell a similar story. The most dramatic version of "Shallow," when Gaga's character first performs for a huge audience, was filmed live at the Greek Theatre in Los Angeles before several thousand adoring Gaga fans.

Intro

Moderately slow

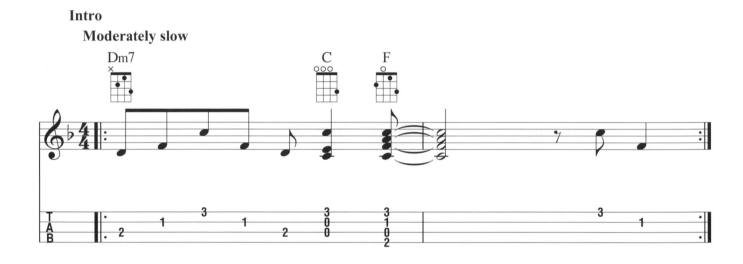

Verse

1. Tell me some-thin' girl, _____ are you hap-py in this
2. Tell me some-thin' boy. _____ Aren't you tired _____ try'n' to

Bridge

D.S. al Coda   ⊕**Coda**

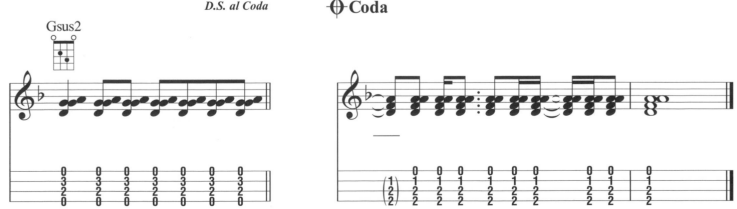

Shallow

from A STAR IS BORN

Words and Music by Stefani Germanotta, Mark Ronson, Andrew Wyatt and Anthony Rossomando

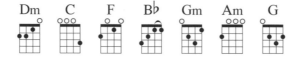

Verse 1

Dm   C   F   B♭   F   C
Tell me somethin', girl, are you happy in this modern world?
Dm   C F B♭   F C
Or do you need more? Is there somethin' else you're searchin' for?
Dm C F B♭   F   C
I'm fall - ing. In all the good times I find myself
        Dm C F   B♭   F   C
Longin'   for change, and in the bad times I fear myself.

Verse 2

Dm   C   F B♭   F   C
Tell me somethin', boy. Aren't you tired try'n' to fill that void?
Dm   C F B♭   F   C
Or do you need more? Ain't it hard keeping it so hard - core?
Dm C F B♭   F   C
I'm   fall - ing. In all the good times I find myself
        Dm C F   B♭   F   C
Longin'   for change, and in the bad times I fear myself.

Chorus 1

Gm   C   F   C Dm
I'm off the deep end, watch as I dive in. I'll never meet the ground.
Gm   F C   F   C Dm
Crash through the surface, where they can't hurt us. We're far from the shallow now.
Gm   C   F   C   Dm
In the sha - ha - sha - ha - low, in the sha - ha - sha - la - la - la - low.
Gm   C   F   C Dm
In the sha - ha - sha - ha - low, we're far from the shallow now.

Bridge

Am   C G   Dm Am C G
Ooh, ha - a - ah - ah, ah, hah ah, ah, ah, ah, ah!

Chorus 2   Repeat Chorus 1

Speak Softly, Love

(Love Theme)

from the Paramount Picture THE GODFATHER
Words by Larry Kusik
Music by Nino Rota

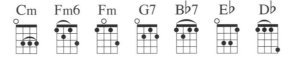

Cm   Fm6   Fm   G7   Bb7   Eb   Db

Verse 1

Cm   Fm6   Cm
Speak softly, love and hold me warm against your heart.
                    Fm
I feel your words, the tender trembling moments start.
     Fm6   Cm
We're in a world, our very own,
   G7   Cm
Sharing a love that only few have ever known.

Bridge

      Bb7   Eb
Wine-colored days warmed by the sun;
     Db   G7
Deep velvet nights when we are one.

Verse 2

Cm   Fm6   Cm
Speak softly, love so no one hears us but the sky.
                 Fm
The vows of love we make will live until we die.
    Fm6   Cm
My life is yours, and all because
   G7   Cm
You came into my world with love so softly, love.

Speak Softly, Love

(Love Theme)

from the Paramount Picture THE GODFATHER
Words by Larry Kusik
Music by Nino Rota

Nino Rota, who wrote film scores for Federico Fellini, Luchino Visconti, and Franco Zefferelli, and many other directors, composed the instrumental "Speak Softly, Love" as a theme for Francis Ford Coppola's 1972 film, *The Godfather*. Larry Kusik, who wrote lyrics for "A Time for Us" and numerous other movie songs, contributed the English words. The film is a classic, and the song — which has been translated into several languages — is highly recognizable.

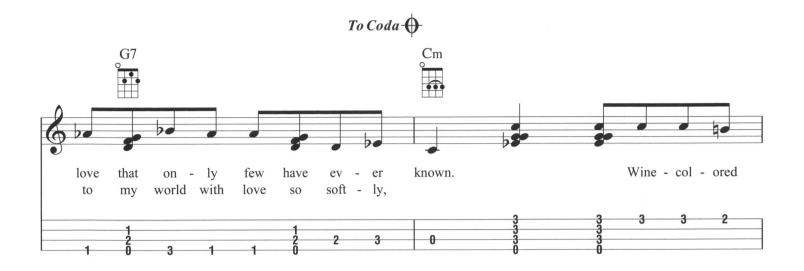

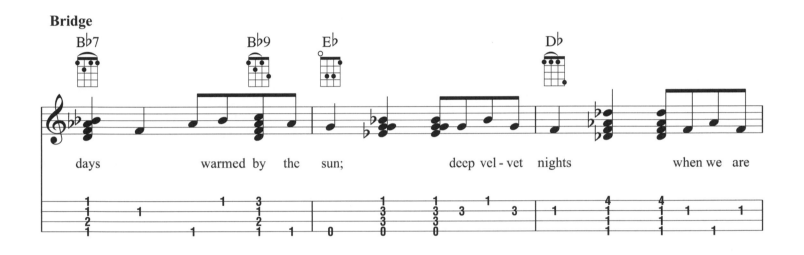

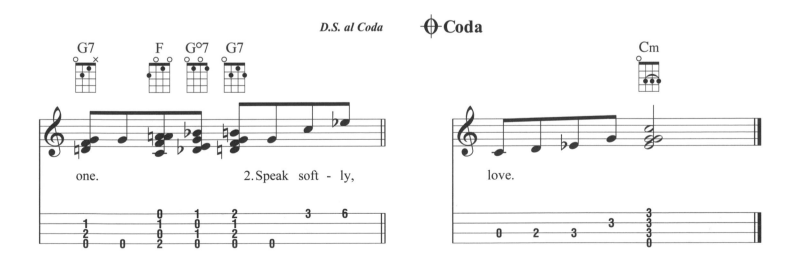

Somewhere, My Love

Lara's Theme from DOCTOR ZHIVAGO

Lyrics by Paul Francis Webster
Music by Maurice Jarre

French composer Maurice-Alexis Jarre has written many notable film scores, including *Lawrence of Arabia*, *Witness*, *Fatal Attraction*, and *Ghost*. Asked by director David Lean to write a song for Lara, a main character in the 1965 film *Doctor Zhivago*, Jarre followed Lean's suggestion to go to the mountains with his girlfriend and write a piece for her. The result was "Lara's Theme," used as a motif throughout the film. Soon after the film's release, three-time Academy Award winner Paul Francis Webster wrote lyrics to the melody and it became "Somewhere, My Love," a much-recorded pop hit.

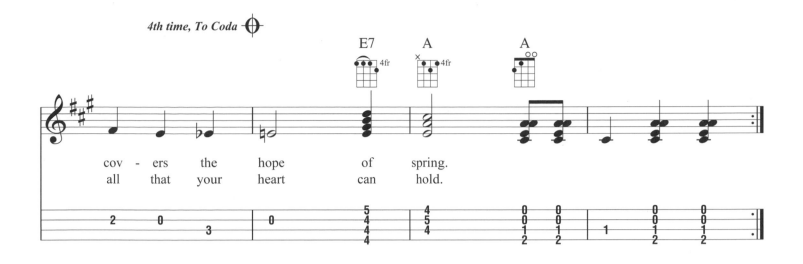

Bridge 1

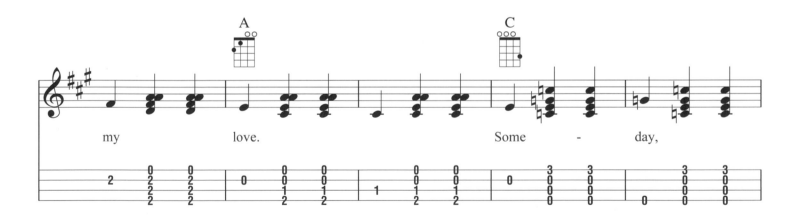

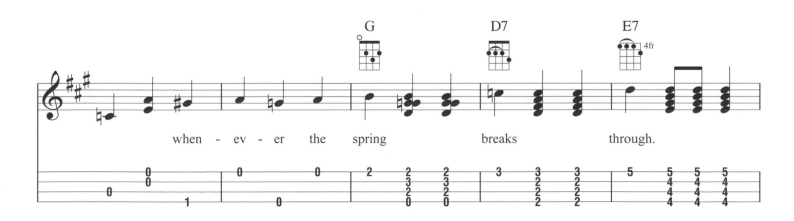

Bridge 2

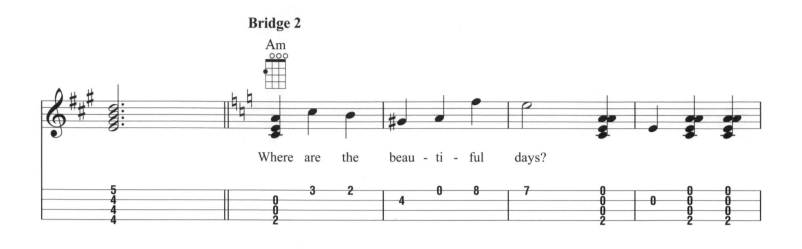

Where are the beau - ti - ful days?

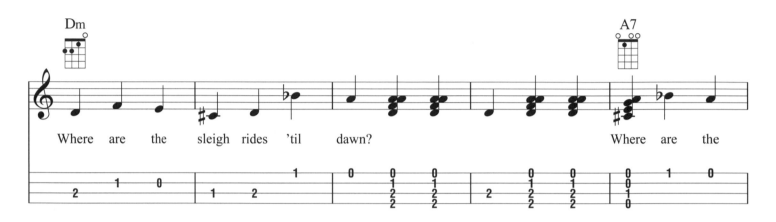

Where are the sleigh rides 'til dawn? Where are the

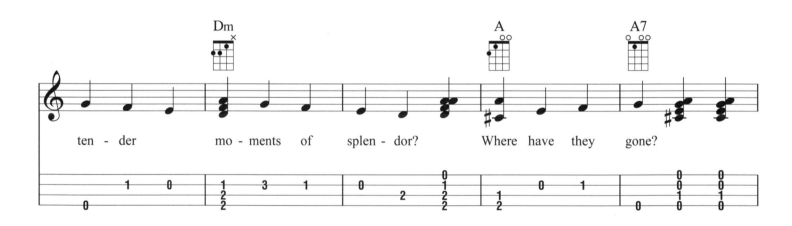

ten - der mo - ments of splen - dor? Where have they gone?

D.C. al Coda
(take repeat)

Coda

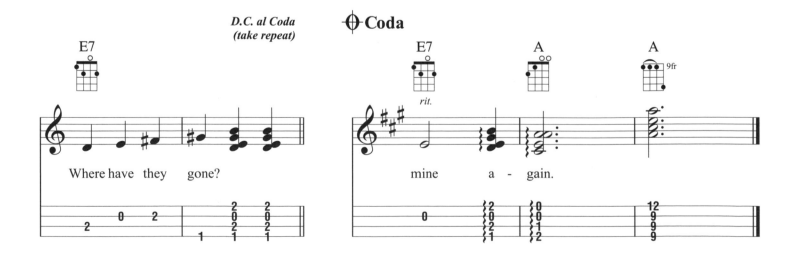

Where have they gone?

mine a - gain.

Somewhere, My Love

Lara's Theme from DOCTOR ZHIVAGO
Lyrics by Paul Francis Webster
Music by Maurice Jarre

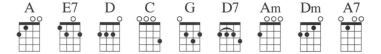

	A E7

Verse 1
 A   E7
Somewhere, my love, there will be songs to sing,
               A
Although the snow covers the hope of spring.
                   E7
Somewhere a hill blossoms in green and gold,
                     A
And there are dreams, all that your heart can hold.

Bridge 1
 D   A
Someday, we'll meet again, my love.
 C   G   D7 E7
Someday, whenever the spring breaks through.

Bridge 2
 Am
Where are the beautiful days?
 Dm
Where are the sleigh rides 'til dawn?
 A7   Dm
Where are the tender moments of splendor?
 A   A7 E7
Where have they gone? Where have they gone?

Verse 2
 A   E7
You'll come to me out of the long ago.
                  A
Warm as the wind, soft as the kiss of snow.
                 E7
'Til then my sweet, think of me now and then.
              A
God speed my love, 'til you are mine again.

Somewhere Out There

from AN AMERICAN TAIL

Music by Barry Mann and James Horner
Lyric by Cynthia Weil

Two mice sang this beautiful pop ballad in Steven Spielberg's 1986 animated film *An American Tail.*
It became a pop hit in the U.S. and several other countries when recorded, at Spielberg's request, by
Linda Ronstadt and James Ingram. Barry Mann and Cynthia Weil, the married couple who gave us
countless hits ("You've Lost That Lovin' Feelin,'" "We Gotta Get Out of This Place," "[You're My]
Soul and Inspiration," "Here You Come Again," "On Broadway," to name just a few) collaborated
with hit singer/songwriter/producer James Ingram to create this song and three others for Spielberg's film.

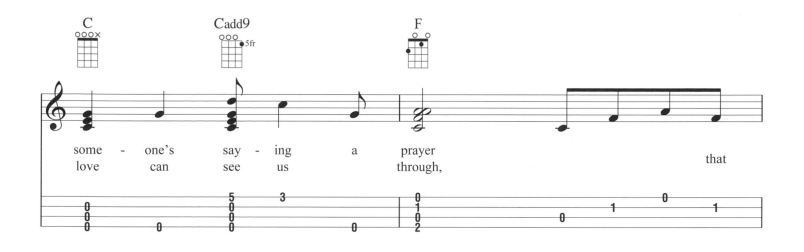

some - one's say - ing a prayer
love can see us through,

that

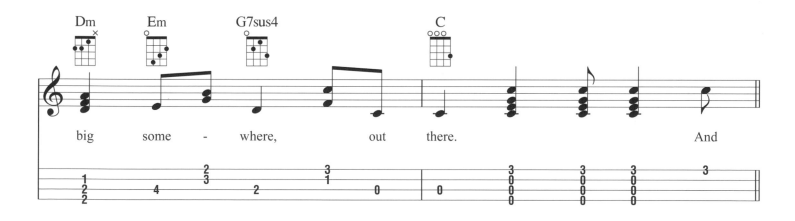

To Coda ⊕

we'll find one an - oth - er, ___ in that
then we'll be to - geth - er ___ some - where

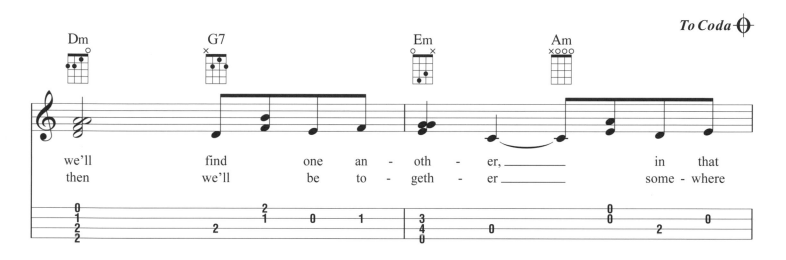

big some - where, out there.

And

Bridge

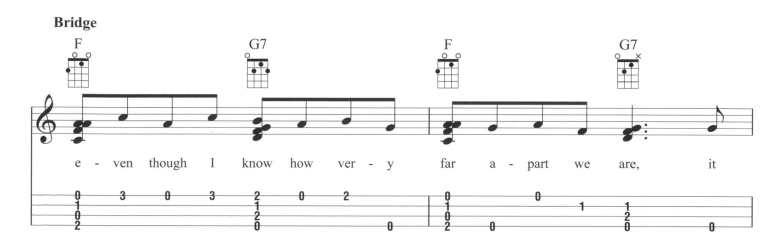

e - ven though I know how ver - y far a - part we are, it

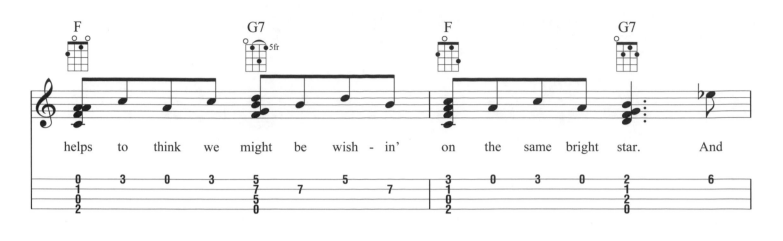

helps   to   think   we   might   be   wish - in'   on   the   same   bright   star.   And

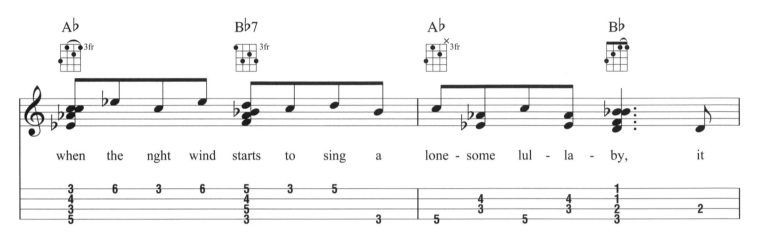

when   the   nght   wind   starts   to   sing   a   lone - some   lul - la - by,   it

D.S. al Coda

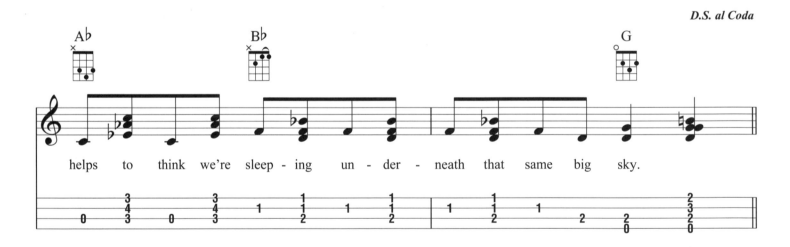

helps   to   think   we're   sleep - ing   un - der - neath   that   same   big   sky.

⊕ Coda

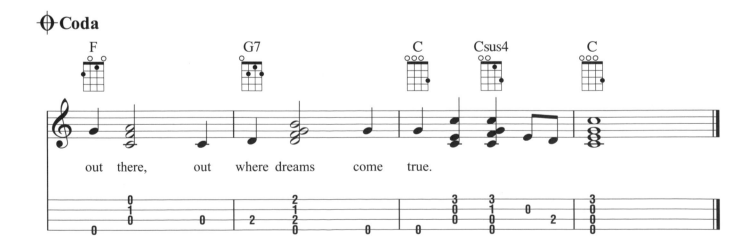

out   there,   out   where   dreams   come   true.

Somewhere Out There

from AN AMERICAN TAIL

Music by Barry Mann and James Horner
Lyric by Cynthia Weil

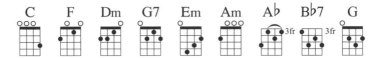

Verse 1
```
   C              F             C              F
Somewhere out there, beneath the pale moonlight,
Dm    G7            Em Am   Dm Em F    G7
Some - one's thinking of   me and lov - ing me tonight.
```

Verse 2
```
   C              F             C              F
Somewhere out there, someone's saying a prayer,
   Dm    G7          Em Am      Dm Em   G7          C
That we'll find one an - oth - er, in that big some - where, out there.
```

Bridge
```
      F           G7          F           G7
And even though I know how very far apart we are,
      F           G7            F              G7
It helps to think we might be wishin' on the same bright star.
      Ab               Bb7          Ab             Bb7
And when the night wind starts to sing a lonesome lullaby,
      Ab               Bb7                          G
It helps to think we're sleeping underneath the same big sky.
```

Verse 3
```
   C              F             C              F
Somewhere out there, if love can see us through,
Dm  G7         Em Am         F
Then we'll be togeth - er, somewhere out there,
   G7               C
Out where dreams come true.
```

Song from M*A*S*H

(Suicide Is Painless)
from M*A*S*H
Words and Music by Mike Altman and Johnny Mandel

Also known as "Suicide Is Painless," this tune was written for the Robert Altman film and the television series, *M*A*S*H*. It was composed by Johnny Mandel (see "The Shadow of Your Smile"), and has become a jazz standard, covered by Bill Evans, Paul Desmond, Bobby Hutcherson, Jimmy Smith, and many others.

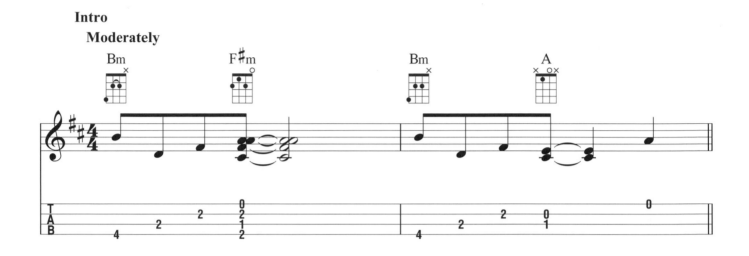

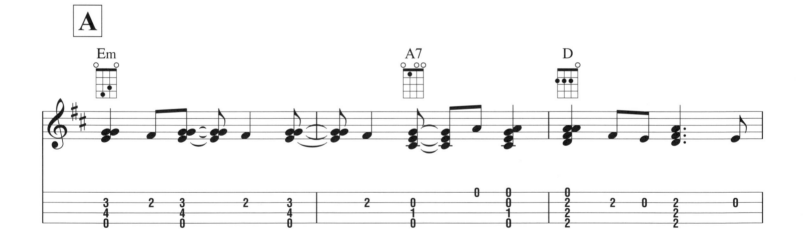

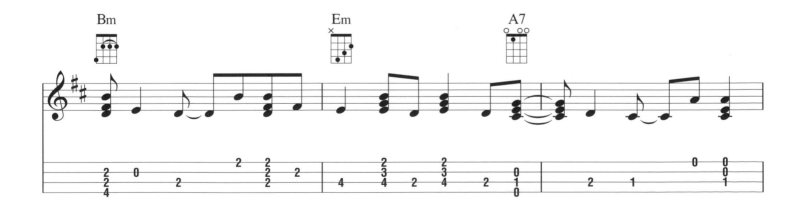

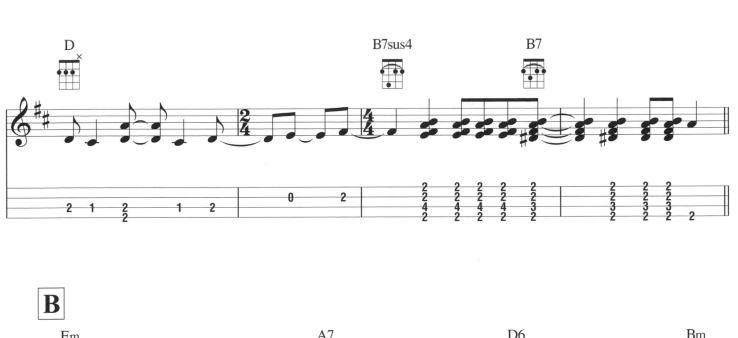

B

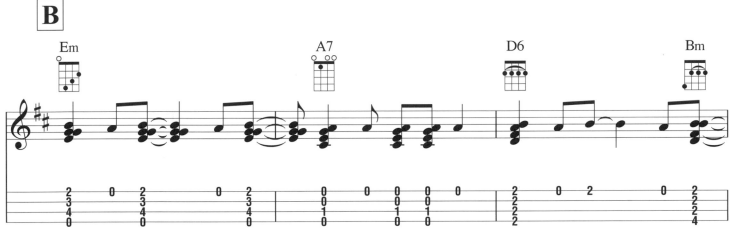

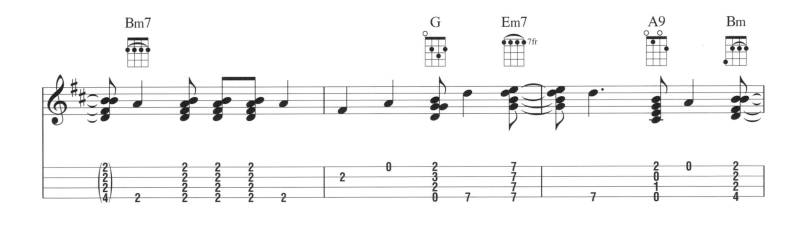

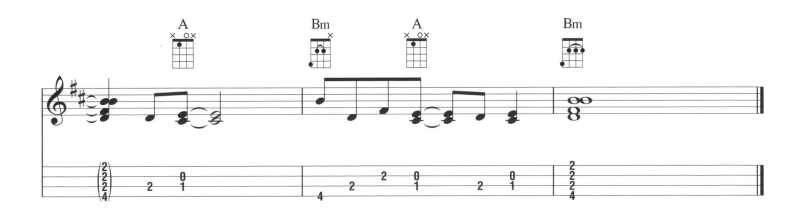

The Way We Were

from the Motion Picture THE WAY WE WERE
Words by Alan and Marilyn Bergman
Music by Marvin Hamlisch

The No. 1 pop hit of 1974, "The Way We Were" was written for the Barbra Streisand/Robert Redford film of the same name. It was composed by Marvin Hamlisch, a famous film composer and one of the few artists to be a "PEGOT" — winner of five prizes: Pulitzer, Emmy, GRAMMY, Oscar, and Tony. The lyrics were penned by Alan and Marilyn Bergman, themselves award-winning composers for film, television, and theater. The song won two Academy Awards for Hamlisch and the two Bergmans.

Coda

Outro

88

The Way We Were

from the Motion Picture THE WAY WE WERE
Words by Alan and Marilyn Bergman
Music by Marvin Hamlisch

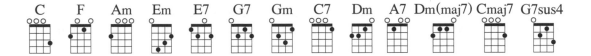

C	F	Am	Em	E7	G7	Gm	C7	Dm	A7	Dm(maj7)	Cmaj7	G7sus4

          C   F   Am C

Verse 1   Memories light the corners of my mind,

               F   Em   E7   Am   C F   G7   C   F

               Misty water-colored memories   of the way we were.

          G7   C   F   Am C

Verse 2   Scattered pictures of the smiles we left behind,

               F   Em   E7 Am C F   G7   C   Gm C7

               Smiles we gave to one another   for the way we were.

          F   Dɪɪɪ   Eɪɪɪ   A7

Bridge   Can it be that it was all so simple then, or has time rewritten every line?

          Dm   Dm(maj7)   F   G7   C   G7

          And if we had the chance to do it all again, tell me, would we, could we?

          C   F   Am C

Verse 3   Memories may be beautiful and yet,

               F   Em   E7 Am   C F   E   Am C

               What's too painful to remember,   we simply choose to forget.

          F   Em   F   Em

Outro   So it's the laughter   we will remember,

          F   Em Dm   G7   Cmaj7 F   G7sus4 Cmaj7

          Whenever we remember   the way we were,   the way we were.

The Windmills of Your Mind

Theme from THE THOMAS CROWN AFFAIR
Words by Alan and Marilyn Bergman
Music by Michel Legrand

French composer Michel Legrand, writer of over 200 film and television scores and winner of three Oscars and five GRAMMYS, set down the music for this song. "What Are You Doing the Rest of Your Life" and "I Will Wait for You" also flowed from his pen. Sung by Noel Harrison in the 1968 film, *The Thomas Crown Affair*, the song won an Academy award. Alan and Marilyn Bergman (see "The Way We Were") wrote the English lyrics used in the film.

The Windmills of Your Mind

Theme from THE THOMAS CROWN AFFAIR
Words by Alan and Marilyn Bergman
Music by Michel Legrand

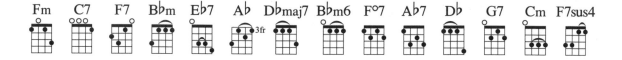

Verse 1

        Fm   C7
Round like a circle in a spiral, like a wheel within a wheel,

                                             Fm
Never ending or beginning on an ever-spinning reel.

                       F7   Bbm
Like a snowball down a mountain, or a carnival balloon,

                    Eb7   Ab
Like a carousel that's turning, running rings around the moon.

                     Dbmaj7   Bbm6
Like a clock whose hands are sweeping past the minutes of its face,

                    C7   F°7
And the world is like an apple whirling silently in space,

                    C7   Fm
Like the circles that you find in the windmills of your mind.

Verse 2

        Fm   C7
Like a tunnel that you follow to a tunnel of its own,

                                             Fm
Down a hollow to a cavern where the sun has never shone,

                       F7   Bbm
Like a door that keeps revolving in a half-forgotten dream,

                    Eb7   Ab
Or the ripples from a pebble someone tosses in a stream.

                     Dbmaj7   Bbm6
Like a clock whose hands are sweeping past the minutes of its face,

                    C7   F°7
And the world is like an apple whirling silently in space,

                    C7   Fm
Like the circles that you find in the windmills of your mind.

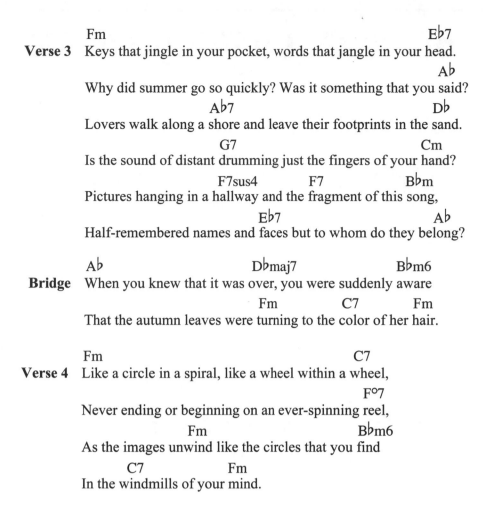

        Fm   Eb7

Verse 3   Keys that jingle in your pocket, words that jangle in your head.

                                                        Ab

Why did summer go so quickly? Was it something that you said?

                Ab7   Db

Lovers walk along a shore and leave their footprints in the sand.

                  G7   Cm

Is the sound of distant drumming just the fingers of your hand?

               F7sus4   F7   Bbm

Pictures hanging in a hallway and the fragment of this song,

                    Eb7   Ab

Half-remembered names and faces but to whom do they belong?

        Ab   Dbmaj7   Bbm6

Bridge   When you knew that it was over, you were suddenly aware

                                Fm   C7   Fm

That the autumn leaves were turning to the color of her hair.

        Fm   C7

Verse 4   Like a circle in a spiral, like a wheel within a wheel,

                                    F°7

Never ending or beginning on an ever-spinning reel,

               Fm   Bbm6

As the images unwind like the circles that you find

      C7   Fm

In the windmills of your mind.

You've Got a Friend in Me

from TOY STORY
Music and Lyrics by Randy Newman

Randy Newman wrote this theme song for the 1995 *Toy Story*; it's heard in all the sequels as well. Nominated for an Academy Award and Golden Globe Award for Best Original Song, it lost to *Pocahontas'* "Colors of the Wind." A prolific singer/songwriter and film composer, Newman also authored the songs for *The Princess and the Frog, Monsters, Inc., Cars,* and all the *Toy Story* movies. He has carried on a family tradition: three of his uncles and four cousins are composers for Hollywood movies. Newman has been nominated for 22 Academy Awards and has won twice.

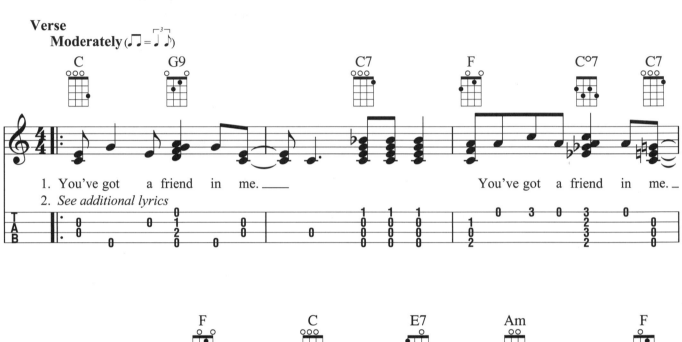

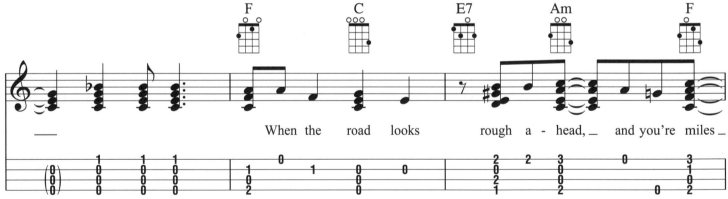

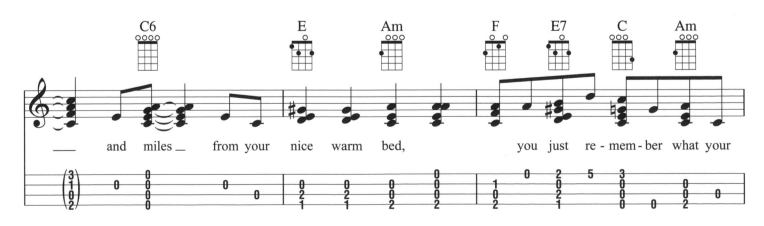

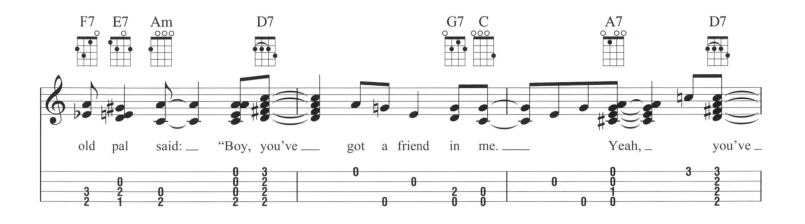

old pal said: __ "Boy, you've __ got a friend in me. __ Yeah, __ you've __

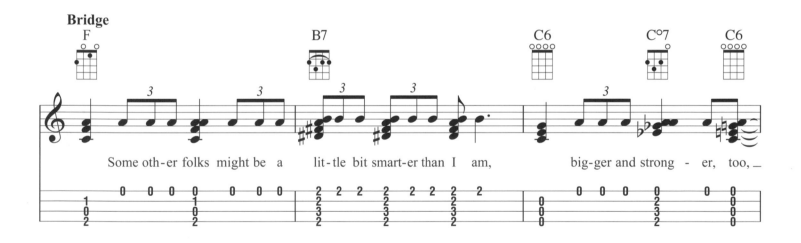

__ got a friend in me." __

Bridge

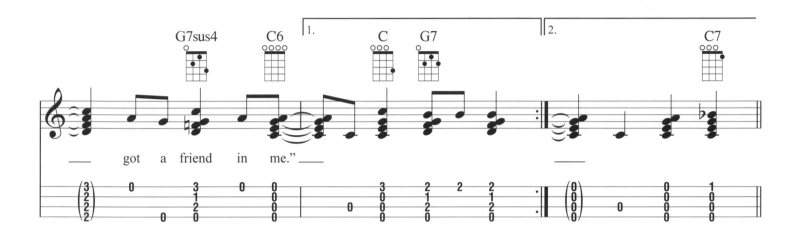

Some oth-er folks might be a lit-tle bit smart-er than I am, big-ger and strong - er, too, __

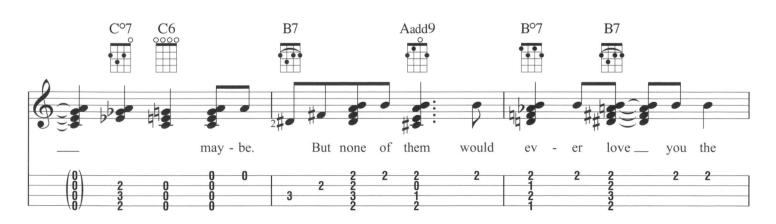

__ may - be. But none of them would ev - er love __ you the

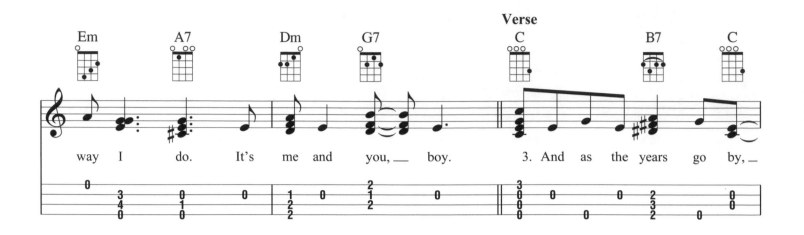

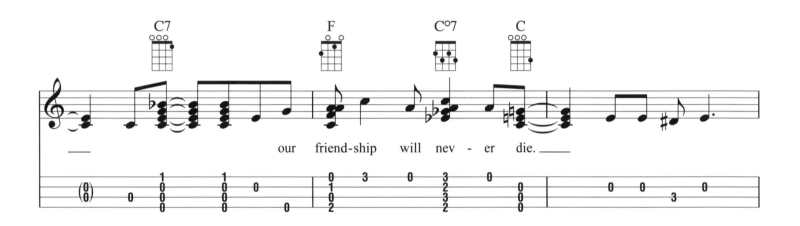

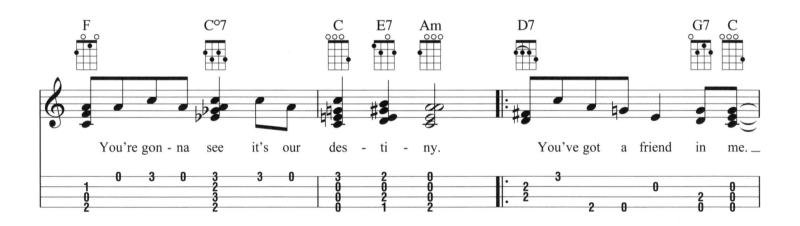

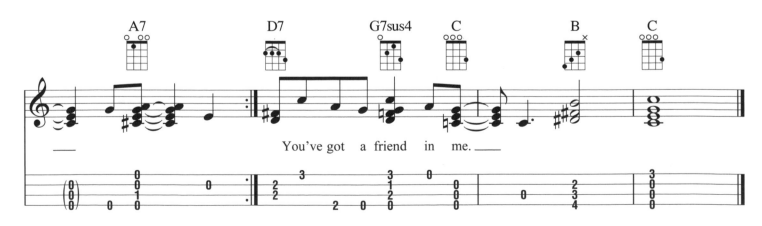

You've Got a Friend in Me

from TOY STORY
Music and Lyrics by Randy Newman

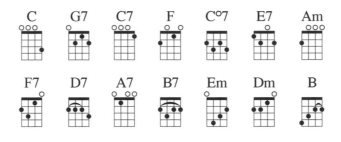

Verse 1

C   G7 C7 F   C°7   C C7
You've got a friend in me. You've got a friend in me.

F   C   E7   Am
When the road looks rough a - head,

      F   C   E7   Am
And you're miles and miles from your nice warm bed,

F E7 C   Am   F7 E7 Am
You just re - member what your old pal said:

     D7   G7   C A7 D7   G7   C   G7
"Boy, you've got a friend in me, yeah, you've got a friend in me."

Verse 2

C   G7 C7 F   C°7   C C7
You've got a friend in me. You've got a friend in me.

F   C   E7   Am
You got troubles and I got 'em too.

F   C   E7   Am
There isn't anything I wouldn't do for you.

F   C   E7 Am
We stick together, we can see it through,

    D7   G7   C A7 D7   G7   C C7
'Cause you've got a friend in me.   You've got a friend in me.

Bridge

F   B7
Some other folks might be a little bit smarter than I am,

C   C°7   C C°7 C
Bigger and stronger too,   maybe.

B7   Em A7 Dm G7
But none of them will ever love you the way I do. It's me and you, boy.

Verse 3

C   G7 C7 F   C°7 C C7
And as the years go by, our friendship will never die.

F   C°7   C E7 Am D7   G7   C A7
You're gonna see it's our des - ti - ny. You've got a friend in me.

D7   G7   C A7 D7   G7   C B C
You've got a friend in me.   You've got a friend in me.

When You Wish Upon a Star

from PINOCCHIO

Words by Ned Washington
Music by Leigh Harline

This is undoubtedly one of the most beautiful popular ballads ever written. Cliff Edwards, a.k.a. "Ukulele Ike," delivered a heart-rending vocal performance, singing in the role of Jiminy Cricket in *Pinocchio* (1940), accompanied by a full orchestra and an angelic backup choir. The first Disney song to win an Oscar, it was written by Leigh Harline and Ned Washington, and has become the general Disney theme. In five countries, it is a standard Christmas song (referring to the Star of Bethlehem). Across the decades, pop singers and jazz artists have enjoyed covering it. Harline also composed music for *Snow White and the Seven Dwarfs*. Disney loved Cliff Edwards, the individual most responsible for the ukulele craze of the 1920s, and hired him for many projects.

When You Wish Upon a Star

from PINOCCHIO
Words by Ned Washington
Music by Leigh Harline

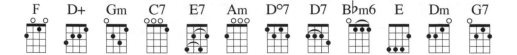

F D+ Gm C7 E7 Am D°7 D7 B♭m6 E Dm G7

	F	D+	Gm	C7			E7 F
Verse 1	When you wish upon a star, makes no difference who you are.

Am D°7   Gm   D7   Gm C7 F C7
Any - thing your heart desires will come to you.

	F	D+	Gm		C7		E7 F
Verse 2	If your heart is in your dream, no request is too extreme.

Am   D°7   Gm D7   Gm   C7 F
When you wish upon a star, as dream - ers do.

B♭m6 C7 F   B♭m6   C7E   F
Bridge Fate   is   kind.   She brings to those who love

Dm   G7   B♭m6 C7
The sweet fulfillment of their secret long - ing.

	F	D+	Gm		C7		E7 F
Verse 3	Like a bolt out of the blue, fate steps in and sees you through.

Am   D°7 Gm D7   Gm   C7   F
When you wish upon a star, your dream comes true.

ABOUT THE AUTHOR

Fred Sokolow is best known as the author of nearly 200 instructional and transcription books and DVDs for ukulele, guitar, banjo, Dobro, mandolin, lap steel, and autoharp. Fred has long been a well-known West Coast multi-string performer and recording artist, particularly on the acoustic music scene. The diverse musical genres covered in his books and DVDs – along with several bluegrass, jazz, and rock CDs he has released – demonstrate his mastery of many musical styles. Whether he's strumming a Tin Pan Alley song on uke, playing Delta bottleneck blues, bluegrass or old-time banjo, '30s swing guitar, or screaming rock solos, he does it with authenticity and passion.

Fred's other ukulele books include:

- *101 Ukulele Tips*, book/soundfiles, **Hal Leonard LLC**
- *Bass Ukulele Method*, book/soundfiles (with Lynn Sokolow), **Hal Leonard LLC**
- *Beatles Fingerstyle Ukulele*, book, **Hal Leonard LLC**
- *Bluegrass Ukulele*, book/CD, **Flea Market Music, distributed by Hal Leonard LLC**
- *Blues Ukulele*, book/CD, **Flea Market Music, distributed by Hal Leonard LLC**
- *Fingerstyle Ukulele*, book/soundfiles, **Hal Leonard LLC**
- *Fretboard Roadmaps for Baritone Ukulele*, book/soundfiles, **Hal Leonard LLC**
- *Fretboard Roadmaps for Ukulele*, book/soundfiles (with Jim Beloff), **Hal Leonard LLC**
- *Jazzing Up the Uke*, book/CD, **Flea Market Music, distributed by Hal Leonard LLC**
- *Ragtime Fingerstyle Ukulele*, book/soundfiles, **Hal Leonard LLC**
- *Slide and Slack Key Ukulele*, book/soundfiles, **Hal Leonard LLC**
- *Disney Songs for Fingerstyle Ukulele*, book, **Hal Leonard LLC**

Email Fred with any questions about this or his other guitar books at: **Sokolowmusic.com**.

UKULELE NOTATION LEGEND

THE MUSICAL STAFF shows pitches and rhythms and is divided by bar lines into measures. Pitches are named after the first seven letters of the alphabet.

TABLATURE graphically represents the ukulele fingerboard. Each horizontal line represents a a string, and each number represents a fret.

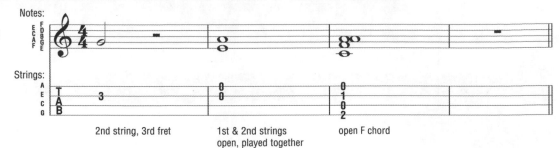

2nd string, 3rd fret | 1st & 2nd strings open, played together | open F chord

HALF-STEP BEND: Strike the note and bend up 1/2 step.

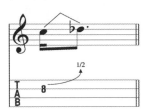

WHOLE-STEP BEND: Strike the note and bend up one step.

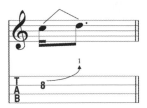

GRACE NOTE BEND: Strike the note and immediately bend up as indicated.

SLIGHT (MICROTONE) BEND: Strike the note and bend up 1/4 step.

BEND AND RELEASE: Strike the note and bend up as indicated, then release back to the original note. Only the first note is struck.

PRE-BEND: Bend the note as indicated, then strike it.

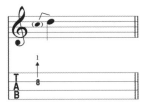

VIBRATO: The string is vibrated by rapidly bending and releasing the note with the fretting hand.

HAMMER-ON: Strike the first (lower) note with one finger, then sound the higher note (on the same string) with another finger by fretting it without picking.

PULL-OFF: Place both fingers on the notes to be sounded. Strike the first note and without picking, pull the finger off to sound the second (lower) note.

LEGATO SLIDE: Strike the first note and then slide the same fret-hand finger up or down to the second note. The second note is not struck.

SHIFT SLIDE: Same as legato slide, except the second note is struck.

TRILL: Very rapidly alternate between the notes indicated by continuously hammering on and pulling off.

TREMOLO PICKING: The note is picked as rapidly and continuously as possible.

NOTE: Tablature numbers in parentheses mean:

1. The note is being sustained over a system (note in standard notation is tied), or

2. The note is sustained, but a new articulation (such as a hammer-on, pull-off, slide or vibrato) begins, or

3. The note is a barely audible "ghost" note (note in standard notation is also in parentheses).

Additional Musical Definitions

	(accent)	• Accentuate note (play it louder)
	(staccato)	• Play the note short
D.S. al Coda		• Go back to the sign (𝄋), then play until the measure marked "***To Coda***," then skip to the section labelled "**Coda**."
D.C. al Fine		• Go back to the beginning of the song and play until the measure marked "***Fine***" (end).
N.C.		• No chord.
		• Repeat measures between signs.
		• When a repeated section has different endings, play the first ending only the first time and the second ending only the second time.